MRS. OVERTHEWAY'S
REMEMBRANCES

JULIANA HORATIA EWING

1st WORLD
LIBRARY
Literary Society

Mrs. Overtheway's Remembrances

Juliana Horatia Ewing

© 1st World Library, 2007
PO Box 2211
Fairfield, IA 52556
www.1stworldlibrary.com
First Edition

LCCN: 2007930831

Softcover ISBN: 978-1-4218-4848-8
Hardcover ISBN: 978-1-4218-4751-1
eBook ISBN: 978-1-4218-4945-4

Purchase *"Mrs. Overtheway's Remembrances"*
as a traditional bound book at:
www.1stWorldLibrary.com/purchase.asp?ISBN= 978-1-4218-4848-8

1st World Library is a literary, educational organization
dedicated to:

- Creating a free internet library of downloadable ebooks

- Hosting writing competitions and offering book publishing
  scholarships.

1ˢᵗ World Library Literary Society

Giving Back to the World

"If you want to work on the core problem, it's early school literacy."

- James Barksdale, former CEO of Netscape

"No skill is more crucial to the future of a child, or to a democratic and prosperous society, than literacy."

- Los Angeles Times

"Literacy... means far more than learning how to read and write... The aim is to transmit... knowledge and promote social participation."

- UNESCO

"Literacy is not a luxury, it is a right and a responsibility. If our world is to meet the challenges of the twenty-first century we must harness the energy and creativity of all our citizens."

- President Bill Clinton

"Parents should be encouraged to read to their children, and teachers should be equipped with all available techniques for teaching literacy, so the varying needs and capacities of individual kids can be taken into account."

- Hugh Mackay

TO MY HUSBAND A.E.

IN REMEMBRANCE OF 1866 AND 1867

J.H.E.

CONTENTS

IDA

... "Thou shall not lack
The flower that's like thy face, pale Primrose."

—CYMBELINE

The little old lady lived over the way, through a green gate that shut with a click, and up three white steps. Every morning at eight o'clock the church bell chimed for Morning Prayer—chim! chime! chim! chime!—and every morning at eight o'clock the little old lady came down the white steps, and opened the gate with a click, and went where the bells were calling.

About this time also little Ida would kneel on a chair at her nursery window in the opposite house to watch the old lady come out and go. The old lady was one of those people who look always the same. Every morning her cheeks looked like faded rose-leaves, and her white hair like a snow-wreath in a garden laughing at the last tea-rose. Every morning she wore the same black satin bonnet, and the same white shawl; had delicate gloves on the smallest of hands, and gathered her skirt daintily up from the smallest of feet. Every morning she carried a clean pocket-handkerchief, and a fresh rose in the same hand with her Prayer-book; and as the Prayer-book, being bound up with the Bible, was very thick, she seemed to have some difficulty in so doing. Every morning, whatever the weather might be, she stood outside the green gate, and looked up at the sky to see if this were clear, and down at the ground to see if that were dry; and so went where the bells were calling.

Ida knew the little old lady quite well by sight, but she did not know her name. Perhaps Ida's great-uncle knew it; but he was a grave, unsociable man, who saw very little of his neighbours, so perhaps he did not; and Ida stood too much in awe of him to trouble him with idle questions. She had once asked Nurse, but Nurse did not know; so the quiet orphan child asked no more. She made up a name for the little old lady herself, however, after the manner of Mr. John Bunyan, and called her Mrs. Overtheway; and morning after morning, though the bread-and-milk breakfast smoked upon the table, she would linger at the window, beseeching—

"One minute more, dear Nurse! Please let me wait till Mrs. Overtheway has gone to church."

And when the little old lady had come out and gone, Ida would creep from her perch, and begin her breakfast. Then, if the chimes went on till half the basinful was eaten, little Ida would nod her head contentedly, and whisper—

"Mrs. Overtheway was in time."

Little Ida's history was a sad one. Her troubles began when she was but a year old, with the greatest of earthly losses— for then her mother died, leaving a sailor husband and their infant child. The sea-captain could face danger, but not an empty home; so he went back to the winds and the waves, leaving his little daughter with relations. Six long years had he been away, and Ida had had many homes, and yet,

Juliana Horatia Ewing

somehow, no home, when one day the postman brought her a large letter, with her own name written upon it in a large hand. This was no old envelope sealed up again—no make-believe epistle to be put into the post through the nursery door: it was a real letter, with a real seal, real stamps, and a great many post-marks; and when Ida opened it there were two sheets written by the Captain's very own hand, in round fat characters, easy to read, with a sketch of the Captain's very own ship at the top, and—most welcome above all!—the news that the Captain's very own self was coming home.

"I shall have a papa all to myself very soon, Nurse," said Ida. "He has written a letter to me, and made me a picture of his ship; it is the 'Bonne Esperance,' which he says means Good Hope. I love this letter better than anything he has ever sent me."

Nevertheless, Ida took out the carved fans and workboxes, the beads, and handkerchiefs, and feathers, the dainty foreign treasures the sailor-father had sent to her from time to time; dusted them, kissed them, and told them that the Captain was coming home. But the letter she wore in her pocket by day, and kept under her pillow by night.

"Why don't you put your letter into one of your boxes, like a tidy young lady, Miss Ida?" said Nurse. "You'll wear it all to bits doing as you do."

"It will last till the ship comes home," said Miss Ida.

It had need then to have been written on the rock, graven with an iron pen for ever; for the "Bonne Esperance" (like other earthly hopes) had perished to return no more. She foundered on her homeward voyage, and went down into the great waters, whilst Ida slept through the stormy night, with the Captain's letter beneath her pillow.

Alas! Alas! Alas!

* * * * *

Two or three months had now passed away since Ida became an orphan. She had become accustomed to the crape-hung frock; she had learnt to read the Captain's letter as the memorial of a good hope which it had pleased God to disappoint; she was fairly happy again. It was in the midst of that new desolation in her lonely life that she had come to stay with her great-uncle, and had begun to watch the doings of the little old lady who lived over the way. When dolls seemed vanity, and Noah's Ark a burden, it had been a quiet amusement, demanding no exertion, to see what little she could see of the old lady's life, and to speculate about what she could not; to wonder and fancy what Mrs. Overtheway looked like without her bonnet, and what she did with herself when she was not at church. Ida's imagination did not carry her far. She believed her friend to be old, immeasurably old, indefinitely old; and had a secret faith that she had never been otherwise. She felt sure that she wore a cap indoors, and that it was a nicer one than Nurse's; that she had real tea, with sugar and cream, instead of milk-and-water, and hot toast rather than bread-and-treacle for tea; that she helped herself at meals, and went to bed according to her own pleasure and convenience; was—perhaps on these very grounds—utterly happy, and had always been so.

"I am only a little girl," said Ida, as she pressed her face sadly to the cold window-pane. "I am only a little girl, and very sad, you know, because Papa was drowned at sea; but Mrs. Overtheway is very old, and always happy, and so I love her."

And in this there was both philosophy and truth.

Juliana Horatia Ewing

It is a mistake to suppose that the happiness of others is always a distasteful sight to the sad at heart. There are times in which life seems shorn of interests and bereaved of pleasure, when it is a relief, almost amounting to consolation, to believe that any one is happy. It is some feeling of this nature, perhaps, which makes the young so attractive to the old. It soothes like the sound of harmonious music, the sight of harmonious beauty. It witnesses to a conviction lying deep even in the most afflicted souls that (come what may), all things were created good, and man made to be blessed; before which sorrow and sighing flee away.

This was one of many things which formed the attraction for Ida in the little old lady who lived over the way. That green gate shut in a life of which the child knew nothing, and which might be one of mysterious delights; to believe that such things could be was consoling, and to imagine them was real entertainment. Ida would sometimes draw a chair quietly to the table beside her own, and fancy that Mrs. Overtheway was having tea with her. She would ask the old lady if she had been in time for church that morning, beg her to take off her bonnet, and apologise politely for the want of hot tea and toast. So far all was well, for Ida could answer any of these remarks on Mrs. Overtheway's behalf; but it may be believed that after a certain point this one-sided conversation flagged. One day Nurse overheard Ida's low murmurs.

"What are you talking about, Miss Ida?" said she.

"I am pretending to have Mrs. Overtheway to tea," said Ida.

"Little girls shouldn't pretend what's not true," replied Nurse, in whose philosophy fancy and falsehood were not distinguished. "Play with your dolls, my dear, and don't move the chairs out of their places."

With which Nurse carried off the chair into a corner as if it had been a naughty child, and Ida gave up her day-dream with a sigh; since to have prolonged the fancy that Mrs. Overtheway was present, she must have imagined her borne off at the crisis of the meal after a fashion not altogether consistent with an old lady's dignity.

Summer passed, and winter came on. There were days when the white steps looked whiter than usual; when the snowdrift came halfway up the little green gate, and the snowflakes came softly down with a persistency which threatened to bury the whole town. Ida knew that on such days Mrs. Overtheway could not go out; but whenever it was tolerably fine the old lady appeared as usual, came daintily down the steps, and went where the bells were calling. Chim! chime! chim! chime! They sounded so near through the frosty air, that Ida could almost have fancied that the church was coming round through the snowy streets to pick up the congregation.

Mrs. Overtheway looked much the same in winter as in summer. She seemed as fresh and lively as ever, carried her Prayer-book and handkerchief in the same hand, was only more warmly wrapped up, and wore fur-lined boots, which were charming. There was one change, however, which went to Ida's heart. The little old lady had no longer a flower to take to church with her. At Christmas she took a sprig of holly, and after that a spray of myrtle, but Ida felt that these were poor substitutes for a rose. She knew that Mrs. Overtheway had flowers somewhere, it is true, for certain pots of forced hyacinths had passed through the little green gate to the Christmas church decorations; but one's winter garden is too precious to be cropped as recklessly as summer rose-bushes, and the old lady went flowerless to church and enjoyed her bulbs at home. But the change went to Ida's heart.

Spring was early that year. At the beginning of February

there was a good deal of snow on the ground, it is true, but the air became milder and milder, and towards the end of the month there came a real spring day, and all the snow was gone.

"You may go and play in the garden, Miss Ida," said Nurse, and Ida went.

She had been kept indoors for a long time by the weather and by a cold, and it was very pleasant to get out again, even when the only amusement was to run up and down the shingly walks and wonder how soon she might begin to garden, and whether the gardener could be induced to give her a piece of ground sufficiently extensive to grow a crop of mustard-and-cress in the form of a capital I. It was the kitchen garden into which Ida had been sent. At the far end it was cut off from the world by an overgrown hedge with large gaps at the bottom, through which Ida could see the high road, a trough for watering horses, and beyond this a wood. The hedge was very thin in February, and Ida had a good view in consequence, and sitting on a stump in the sunshine she peered through the gap to see if any horses came to drink. It was as good as a peep-show, and indeed much better.

"The snow has melted," gurgled the water, "here I am." It was everywhere. The sunshine made the rich green mosses look dry, but in reality they were wet, and so was everything else. Slish! slosh! Put your feet where you would, the water was everywhere. It filled the stone trough, which, being old and grey and steady, kept it still, and bade it reflect the blue sky and the gorgeous mosses; but the trough soon overflowed, and then the water slipped over the side, and ran off in a wayside stream. "Winter is gone!" it spluttered as it ran. "Winter is gone, winter-is-gone, winterisgone!" And, on the principle that a good thing cannot be said too often, it went on with this all through the summer, till the next winter came and stopped its mouth with icicles. As the stream chattered, so the birds in the wood sang—Tweet! tweet! chirrup! throstle! Spring! Spring! Spring!—and they twittered from tree to tree, and shook the bare twigs with melody; whilst a single blackbird sitting still upon a bough below, sang "Life!" "Life!" "Life!" with the loudest pipe of his throat, because on such a day it was happiness only to be alive.

It was like a wonderful fairy-tale, to which Ida listened with clasped hands.

Presently another song came from the wood: it was a hymn sung by children's voices, such as one often hears carolled by a troop of little urchins coming home from school. The words fell familiarly on Ida's ears:

"Quite through the streets with silver sound,
The flood of life doth flow;
Upon whose banks on every side
The wood of life doth grow.

"Thy gardens and thy gallant walks
Continually are green;
There grow such sweet and pleasant flowers
As nowhere else are seen.

"There trees for evermore bear fruit,
And evermore do spring;
There evermore the Angels sit,
And evermore do sing."

Here the little chorus broke off, and the children came pouring out of the wood with chattering and laughter. Only one lingered, playing under a tree, and finishing the song. The child's voice rose shrill and clear like that of the

Juliana Horatia Ewing

blackbird above him. He also sang of Life—Eternal life—knowing little more than the bird of the meaning of his song, and having little less of that devotion of innocence in which happiness is praise.

But Ida had ceased to listen to the singing. Her whole attention was given to the children as they scampered past the hedge, dropping bits of moss and fungi and such like woodland spoil. For, tightly held in the grubby hands of each—plucked with reckless indifference to bud and stalk, and fading fast in their hot prisons—were primroses. Ida started to her feet, a sudden idea filling her brain. The birds were right, Spring had come, and there were flowers—*flowers for Mrs. Overtheway.*

Ida was a very quiet, obedient little girl, as a general rule; indeed, in her lonely life she had small temptation to pranks or mischief of any kind. She had often been sent to play in the back garden before, and had never thought of straying beyond its limits; but to-day a strong new feeling had been awakened by the sight of the primroses.

"The hole is very large," said Ida, looking at the gap in the hedge; "if that dead root in the middle were pulled up, it would be wonderfully large."

She pulled the root up, and, though wonderful is a strong term, the hole was certainly larger.

"It is big enough to put one's head through," said Ida, and, stooping down, she exemplified the truth of her observation.

"Where the head goes, the body will follow," they say, and Ida's little body was soon on the other side of the hedge; the adage says nothing about clothes, however, and part of Ida's dress was left behind. It had caught on the stump as she scrambled through. But accidents will happen, and she was in the road, which was something.

"It is like going into the world to seek one's fortune," she thought; "thus Gerda went to look for little Kay, and so Joringel sought for the enchanted flower. One always comes to a wood."

And into the wood she came. Dame Nature had laid down her new green carpets, and everything looked lovely; but, as has been before said, it certainly was damp. The little singer under the tree cared no more for this, however, than the blackbird above him.

"Will you tell me, please, where you got your primroses?" asked Ida.

The child made a quaint, half-military salute; and smiled.

"Yonder," he said laconically, and, pointing up the wood, he went on with the song that he could not understand:

> "Ah, my sweet home, Jerusalem,
> Would God I were in thee!
> Would God my woes were at an end,
> Thy joys that I might see!"

Ida went on and on, looking about her as she ran. Presently the wood sloped downwards, and pretty steeply, so that it was somewhat of a scramble; yet still she kept a sharp look-out, but no primroses did she see, except a few here and there upon the ground, which had been plucked too close to their poor heads to be held in anybody's hands. These showed the way, however, and Ida picked them up in sheer pity and carried them with her.

"This is how Hop-o'-my-Thumb found his way home," she thought.

At the bottom of the hill ran a little brook, and on the opposite side of the brook was a bank, and on the top of the bank was a hedge, and under the hedge were the primroses. But the brook was between!

Ida looked and hesitated. It was too wide to jump across, and here, as elsewhere, there was more water than usual. To turn back, however, was out of the question. Gerda would not have been daunted in her search by coming to a stream, nor would any one else that ever was read of in fairy tales. It is true that in Fairy-land there are advantages which cannot always be reckoned upon by commonplace children in this commonplace world. When the straw, the coal, and the bean came to a rivulet in their travels, the straw laid himself across as a bridge for the others, and had not the coal been a degree too hot on that unlucky occasion, they might (for anything Ida knew to the contrary) still have been pursuing their journey in these favourable circumstances. But a travelling-companion who expands into a bridge on an emergency is not to be met with every day; and as to poor Ida—she was alone. She stood first on one leg, and then on the other, she looked at the water, and then at the primroses, and then at the water again, and at last perceived that in one place there was a large, flat, moss-covered stone in the middle of the stream, which stood well out of the water, and from which—could she but reach it—she might scramble to the opposite bank. But how to reach it? that nice, large, secure, comfortable-looking stone.

"I must put some more stones," thought Ida. There were plenty in the stream, and Ida dragged them up, and began to make a ford by piling them together. It was chilly work, for a cloud had come over the sun; and Ida was just a little bit frightened by the fresh-water shrimps, and some queer, many-legged beasts, who shot off the stones as she lifted them. At last the ford was complete. Ida stepped daintily over the bridge she had made, and jumped triumphantly on to the big stone. Alas! for trusting to appearances. The stone that looked so firm, was insecurely balanced below, and at the first shock one side went down with a splash, and Ida went with it. What a triumph for the shrimps! She scrambled to the bank, however, made up a charming bunch of primroses, and turned to go home. Never mind how she got back across the brook. We have all waded streams before now, and very good fun it is in June, but rather chilly work in February; and, in spite of running home, Ida trembled as much with cold as with excitement when she stood at last before Mrs. Overtheway's green gate.

Click! Ida went up the white steps, marking them sadly with her wet feet, and gave a valiant rap. The door was opened, and a tall, rather severe-looking housekeeper asked:

"What do you want, my dear?"

A shyness, amounting to terror, had seized upon Ida, and she could hardly find voice to answer.

"If you please, I have brought these for—"

For whom? Ida's pale face burnt crimson as she remembered that after all she did not know the little old lady's name. Perhaps the severe housekeeper was touched by the sight of the black frock, torn as it was, for she said kindly:

"Don't be frightened, my dear. What do you want?"

"These primroses," said Ida, who was almost choking. "They are for Mrs. Overtheway to take to church with her. I am very sorry, if you please, but I don't know her name, and I call her Mrs. Overtheway because, you know, she lives over the way. At least—" Ida added, looking back across the road with a sudden confusion in her ideas, "at least—I mean—you know—*we* live over the way." And overwhelmed with shame at her own stupidity, Ida stuffed the flowers into the woman's hand, and ran home as if a lion were at her heels.

"Well! Miss Ida," began Nurse, as Ida opened the nursery door (and there was something terrible in her "well"); "if I ever—" and Nurse seized Ida by the arm, which was generally premonitory of her favourite method of punishment—"a good shaking." But Ida clung close and flung her arms round Nurse's neck.

"Don't shake me, Nursey, dear," she begged, "my head aches so. I have been very naughty, I know. I've done everything you can think of; I've crept through the hedge, and been right through the wood, and made a ford, and tumbled into the brook, and waded back, and run all the way home, and been round by the town for fear you should see me. And I've done something you could never, never think of if you tried till next Christmas, I've got some flowers for Mrs. Overtheway, only I did it so stupidly; she will think me a perfect goose, and perhaps be angry," and the tears came into Ida's eyes.

"She'll think you a naughty, troublesome child, as you are," said Nurse, who seldom hesitated to assume the responsibility of any statement that appeared to be desirable; "you're mad on that old lady, I think. Just look at that dress!"

Ida looked, but her tears were falling much too fast for her to have a clear view of anything, and the torn edges of the rent seemed fringed with prismatic colours.

To crown all she was sent to bed. In reality, this was to save the necessity of wearing her best frock till the other was mended, and also to keep her warm in case she should have caught cold; but Nurse spoke of it as a punishment, and Ida wept accordingly. And this was a triumph of that not uncommon line of nursery policy which consists in elaborately misleading the infant mind for good.

Chim! chime! went the bells next morning, and Mrs. Overtheway came down the white steps and through the green gate with a bunch of primroses in her hand. She looked up as usual, but not to the sky. She looked to the windows of the houses over the way, as if she expected some one to be looking for her. There was no face to be seen, however; and in the house directly opposite, one of the upper blinds was drawn down. Ida was ill.

How long she was ill, and of what was the matter with her, Ida had no very clear idea. She had visions of toiling through the wood over and over again, looking vainly for something that could never be found; of being suddenly surrounded and cut off by swollen streams; and of crawling, unclean beasts with preternatural feelers who got into her boots. Then these heavy dreams cleared away in part, and the stream seemed to ripple like the sound of church bells, and these chimed out the old tune

"Quite through the streets, with silver sound," &c.

And then, at last, she awoke one fine morning to hear the sweet chim-chiming of the church bells, and to see Nurse sitting by her bedside. She lay still for a few moments to make quite sure, and then asked in a voice so faint that it surprised herself:

"Has Mrs. Overtheway gone to church?"

Juliana Horatia Ewing

On which, to her great astonishment, Nurse burst into tears. For this was the first reasonable sentence that poor Ida had spoken for several days.

To be very ill is not pleasant; but the slow process of getting back strength is often less pleasant still. One afternoon Ida knelt in her old place at the window. She was up, but might not go out, and this was a great grief. The day had been provokingly fine, and even now, though the sun was setting, it seemed inclined to make a fresh start, so bright was the rejuvenated glow with which it shone upon the opposite houses, and threw a mystic glory over Mrs. Overtheway's white steps and green railings. Oh! how Ida had wished to go out that afternoon! How long and clear the shadows were! It seemed to Ida that whoever was free to go into the open air could have nothing more to desire. "Out of doors" looked like Paradise to the drooping little maid, and the passers-by seemed to go up and down the sunny street in a golden dream. Ida gazed till the shadows lengthened, and crept over the street and up the houses; till the sunlight died upon the railings, and then upon the steps, and at last lingered for half an hour in bright patches among the chimney-stacks, and then went out altogether, and left the world in shade.

Twilight came on and Ida sat by the fire, which rose into importance now that the sunshine was gone; and, moreover, spring evenings are cold.

Ida felt desolate, and, on the whole, rather ill-used. Nurse had not been upstairs for hours, and though she had promised real tea and toast this evening, there were no signs of either as yet. The poor child felt too weak to play, and reading made her eyes ache. If only there were some one to tell her a story.

It grew dark, and then steps came outside the door, and a fumbling with the lock which made Ida nervous.

"Do come in, Nursey!" she cried.

The door opened, and someone spoke; but the voice was not the voice of Nurse. It was a sweet, clear, gentle voice; musical, though no longer young; such a voice as one seldom hears and never forgets, which came out of the darkness, saying:

"It is not Nurse, my dear; she is making the tea, and gave me leave to come up alone. I am Mrs. Overtheway."

And there in the firelight stood the little old lady, as she has been before described, except that instead of her Prayer-book she carried a large pot hyacinth in her two hands.

"I have brought you one of my pets, my dear," said she. "I think we both love flowers."

The little old lady had come to tea. This was charming. She took off her bonnet, and her cap more than fulfilled Ida's expectations, although it was nothing smarter than a soft mass of tulle, tied with white satin strings. But what a face looked out of it! Mrs. Overtheway's features were almost perfect. The beauty of her eyes was rather enhanced by the blue shadows that Time had painted round them, and they were those good eyes which remind one of a clear well, at the bottom of which he might see truth. When young she must have been exquisitely beautiful, Ida thought. She was lovely still.

In due time Nurse brought up tea, and Ida could hardly believe that her fancies were realized at last; indeed more than realized—for no bread and treacle diminished the dignity of the entertainment; and Nurse would as soon have thought of carrying off the Great Mogul on his cushions, as of putting Mrs. Overtheway and her chair into the corner.

But there is a limit even to the space of time for which one can enjoy tea and buttered toast. The tray was carried off, the hyacinth put in its place, and Ida curled herself up in an easy chair on one side of the fire, Mrs. Overtheway being opposite.

"You see I am over the way still," laughed the little old lady. "Now, tell me all about the primroses." So Ida told everything, and apologized for her awkward speeches to the housekeeper.

"I don't know your name yet," said she.

"Call me Mrs. Overtheway still, my dear, if you please," said the little old lady. "I like it."

So Ida was no wiser on this score.

"I was so sorry to hear that you had been made ill on my account," said Mrs. Overtheway. "I have been many times to ask after you, and to-night I asked leave to come to tea. I wish I could do something to amuse you, you poor little invalid. I know you must feel dull."

Ida's cheeks flushed.

"If you would only tell me a story," she said, "I do so like hearing Nurse's stories. At least she has only one, but I like it. It isn't exactly a story either, but it is about what happened in her last place. But I am rather tired of it. There's Master Henry—I like him very much, he was always in mischief; and there's Miss Adelaide, whose hair curled naturally—at least with a damp brush—I like her; but I don't have much of them; for Nurse generally goes off about a quarrel she had with the cook, and I never could tell what they quarrelled about, but Nurse said cook was full of malice and deceitfulness, so she left. I'm rather tired of it."

"What sort of a story shall I tell you?" asked Mrs. Overtheway.

"A true one, I think," said Ida. "Something that happened to you yourself, if you please. You must remember a great many things, being so old."

And Ida said this in simple good-faith, believing it to be a compliment.

"It is quite true," said Mrs. Overtheway, "that one remembers many things at the end of a long life, and that they are often those things which happened a long while ago, and which are sometimes so slight in themselves that it is wonderful that they should not have been forgotten. I remember, for instance, when I was about your age, an incident that occurred which gave me an intense dislike to a special shade of brown satin. I hated it then, and at the end of more than half a century, I hate it still. The thing in itself was a mere folly; the people concerned in it have been dead for many years, and yet at the present time I should find considerable difficulty in seeing the merits of a person who should dress in satin of that peculiar hue.

"What was it?" asked Ida.

"It was not amber satin, and it was not snuff-coloured satin; it was one of the shades of brown known by the name of feuille-morte, or dead-leaf colour. It is pretty in itself, and yet I dislike it."

"How funny," said Ida, wriggling in the arm-chair with satisfaction. "Do tell me about it."

"But it is not funny in the least, unfortunately," said Mrs. Overtheway, laughing. "It isn't really a story, either. It is not even like Nurse's experiences. It is only a strong remembrance of my childhood, that isn't worth repeating, and could hardly amuse you."

"Indeed, indeed, it would," said Ida. "I like the sound of it. Satin is so different from cooks."

Mrs. Overtheway laughed.

"Still, I wish I could think of something more entertaining," said she.

"Please tell me that," said Ida, earnestly; "I would rather hear something about you than anything else."

There was no resisting this loving argument. Ida felt she had gained her point, and curled herself up into a listening attitude accordingly. The hyacinth stood in solemn sweetness as if it were listening also; and Mrs. Overtheway, putting her little feet upon the fender to warm, began the story of—

MRS. MOSS

"It did not move my grief, to see
The trace of human step departed,
Because the garden was deserted,
The blither place for me!

"Friends, blame me not! a narrow ken
Hath childhood 'twixt the sun and sward:
We draw the moral afterward—
We feel the gladness then."

—E. BARRETT BROWNING

"I remember," said Mrs. Overtheway, "old as I am, I remember distinctly many of the unrecognized vexations, longings, and disappointments of childhood. By unrecognized, I mean those vexations, longings, and disappointments which could not be understood by nurses, are not confided even to mothers, and through which, even in our cradles, we become subject to that law of humanity which gives to every heart its own secret bitterness to be endured alone. These are they which sometimes outlive weightier memories, and produce life-long impressions disproportionate to their value; but oftener, perhaps, are washed away by the advancing tide of time—the vexations, longings, and disappointments of the next period of our lives. These are they which are apt to be forgotten too soon to benefit our children, and which in the forgetting make childhood all bright to look back upon, and foster that happy fancy that there is one division of mortal life in which greedy desire, unfulfilled purpose, envy, sorrow, weariness and satiety, have no part, by which every man believes himself at least to have been happy as a child.

"My childhood, on the whole, was a very happy one. The story that I am about to relate is only a fragment of it.

"As I look into the fire, and the hot coals shape themselves into a thousand memories of the past, I seem to be staring with childish eyes at a board that stares back at me out of a larch plantation, and gives notice that 'This House is to Let.' Then, again, I seem to peep through rusty iron gates at the house itself—an old red house, with large windows, through which one could see the white shutters that were always closed. To look at this house, though only with my mind's eye, recalls the feeling of mysterious interest with which I looked at it fifty years ago, and brings back the almost oppressive happiness of a certain day, when Sarah, having business with the couple who kept the empty manor, took me with her, and left me to explore the grounds whilst she visited her friends.

"Next to a companion with that rare sympathy of mind to mind, that exceptional coincidence of tastes, which binds some few friendships in a chain of mesmeric links, supplanting all the complacencies of love by intuition, is a companion whose desires and occupations are in harmony, if not in unison, with one's own. That friend whom the long patience of the angler does not chafe, the protracted pleasures of the sketcher do not weary, because time flies as swiftly with him whilst he pores over his book, or devoutly seeks botanical specimens through the artist's middle distance; that friend, in short—that valuable friend—who is blessed with the great and good quality of riding a hobby of his own, and the greater and better quality of allowing other people to ride theirs.

"I did not think out all this fifty years ago, neither were the tastes of that excellent housemaid, Sarah, quite on a level with those of which I have spoken; but I remember feeling the full comfort of the fact that Sarah's love for friendly gossip was quite as ardent as mine for romantic discovery; that she was disposed to linger quite as long to chat as I to explore; and that she no more expected me to sit wearily through her kitchen confidences, than I imagined that she would give a long afternoon to sharing my day-dreams in the gardens of the deserted manor.

"We had ridden our respective hobbies till nearly tea-time before she appeared."

"'I'm afraid you must be tired of waiting, Miss Mary,' said she."

"'Tired!' I exclaimed, 'not in the least. I have been so happy, and I am so much obliged to you, Sarah.'"

"Need I say why I was so happy that afternoon? Surely most people have felt—at least in childhood—the fascination of deserted gardens, uninhabited houses, ruined churches. They have that advantage over what is familiar and in use that undiscovered regions have over the comfortable one that the traveller leaves to explore them, that the secret which does not concern me has over the facts which do, that what we wish for has over what we possess.

"If you, my dear, were to open one of those drawers, and find Nurse's Sunday dress folded up in the corner, it would hardly amuse you; but if, instead thereof, you found a dress with a long stiff bodice, square at the neck, and ruffled round the sleeves, such as you have seen in old pictures, no matter how old or useless it might be, it would shed round it an atmosphere of delightful and mysterious speculations. This curiosity, these fancies, roused by the ancient dress, whose wearer has passed away, are awakened equally by empty houses where someone must once have lived, though his place knows him no more. It was so with the manor. How often had I peeped through the gates, catching sight of garden walks, and wondering whither they led, and who had walked in them; seeing that the shutters behind one window were partly open, and longing to look in.

"To-day I had been in the walks and peeped through the window. This was the happiness.

"Through the window I had seen a large hall with a marble floor and broad stone stairs winding upwards into unknown regions. By the walks I had arrived at the locked door of the kitchen garden, at a small wood or wilderness of endless delights (including a broken swing), and at a dilapidated summer-house. I had wandered over the spongy lawn, which was cut into a long green promenade by high clipt yew-hedges, walking between which, in olden times, the ladies grew erect and stately, as plants among brushwood stretch up to air and light.

"Finally, I had brought away such relics as it seemed to me that honesty would allow. I had found half a rusty pair of scissors in the summer-house. Perhaps some fair lady of former days had lost them here, and swept distractedly up and down the long walks seeking them. Perhaps they were a present, and she had given a luck-penny for them, lest they should cut love. Sarah said the housekeeper might have dropped them there; but Sarah was not a person of sentiment.

I did not show her the marble I found by the hedge, the acorn I picked up in the park, nor a puny pansy which, half way back to a wild heartsease, had touched me as a pathetic memorial of better days. When I got home, I put the scissors, the marble, and the pansy into a box. The acorn I hung in a bottle of water—it was to be an oak tree.

"Properly speaking, I was not at home just then, but on a visit to my grandmother and a married aunt without children who lived with her. A fever had broken out in my own home, and my visit here had been prolonged to keep me out of the way of infection. I was very happy and comfortable except for one single vexation, which was this:

"I slept on a little bed in what had once been the nursery, a large room which was now used as a workroom. A great deal of sewing was done in my grandmother's house, and the sewing-maid and at least one other of the servants sat there every evening. A red silk screen was put before my bed to shield me from the candlelight, and I was supposed to be asleep when they came upstairs. But I never remember to have been otherwise than wide awake, nervously awake, wearily awake. This was the vexation. I was not a strong child, and had a very excitable brain; and the torture that it was to hear those maids gossiping on the other side of the dim red light of my screen I cannot well describe, but I do most distinctly remember. I tossed till the clothes got hot, and threw them off till I got cold, and stopped my ears, and pulled the sheet over my face, and tried not to listen, and listened in spite of all. They told long stories, and made many jokes that I couldn't understand; sometimes I heard names that I knew, and fancied I had learnt some wonderful secret. Sometimes, on the contrary, I made noises to intimate that I was awake, when one of them would rearrange my glaring screen, and advise me to go to sleep; and then they talked in whispers, which was more distracting still.

Juliana Horatia Ewing

"One evening—some months after my ramble round the manor—the maids went out to tea, and I lay in peaceful silence watching the shadows which crept noiselessly about the room as the fire blazed, and wishing Sarah and her colleagues nothing less than a month of uninterrupted tea-parties. I was almost asleep when Aunt Harriet came into the room. She brought a candle, put up my screen (the red screen again!), and went to the work-table. She had not been rustling with the work things for many minutes when my grandmother followed her, and shut the door with an air which seemed to promise a long stay. She also gave a shove to my screen, and then the following conversation began:

"'I have been to Lady Sutfield's to-day, Harriet.'"

"'Indeed, ma'am.' But my aunt respectfully continued her work, as I could hear by the scraping of the scissors along the table."

"'I heard some news there. The manor is let.'"

"I almost jumped in my bed, and Aunt Harriet's scissors paused."

"'Let, ma'am! To whom!'"

"'To a Mrs. Moss. You must have heard me speak of her. I knew her years ago, when we were both young women. Anastatia Eden, she was then.'"

"I could hear my aunt move to the fire, and sit down."

"'The beautiful Miss Eden? Whom did she marry at last? Was there not some love-affair of hers that you knew about?'"

"'Her love-affairs were endless. But you mean Mr. Sandford. She treated him very ill—very ill.'"

"There was a pause, while the fire crackled in the silence; and then, to the infinite satisfaction of my curiosity, Aunt Harriet said:

"'I've forgotten the story, ma'am. He was poor, was he not?'"

"'He had quite enough to marry on,' my grandmother answered, energetically; 'but he was not a great match. It was an old story, my dear. The world! The world! The world! I remember sitting up with Anastatia after a ball, where he had been at her side all the evening. We sipped hot posset, and talked of our partners. Ah, dear!' and here my grandmother heaved a sigh; partly, perhaps, because of the follies of youth, and partly, perhaps, because youth had gone, and could come back no more.

"'Anastatia talked of him,' she continued. 'I remember her asking me if "her man" were not a pretty fellow, and if he had not sweet blue eyes and the greatest simplicity I ever knew but in a child. It was true enough; and he was a great deal more than that—a great deal more than she ever understood. Poor Anastatia! I advised her to marry him, but she seemed to look on that as impossible. I remember her saying that it would be different if she were not an acknowledged beauty; but it was expected that she would marry well, and he was comparatively poor, and not even singular. He was accomplished, and the soul of honour, but simple, provokingly simple, with no pretensions to carry off the toast of a county. My dear, if he had been notorious in any way—for dissipation, for brawling, for extravagance—I believe it would have satisfied the gaping world, and he would have had a chance. But there was nothing to talk about, and Anastatia had not the courage to take him for himself. She had the world at her feet, and paid for it by being bound by its opinion.'"

"Here my grandmother, who was apt to moralize, especially when relating biographies of young ladies, gave another sigh."

"'Then why did she encourage him?' inquired Aunt Harriet; who also moralized, but with more of indignation and less of philosophy."

"'I believe she loved him in spite of herself; but at the last, when he offered, she turned prudent and refused him.'"

"'Poor man! Did he ever marry?'"

"'Yes, and very happily—a charming woman. But the strange part of the story is, that he came quite unexpectedly into a large property that was in his family.'"

"'Did he? Then he would have been as good a match as most of her admirers?'"

"'Better. It was a fine estate. Poor Anastatia!'"

"'Serve her right,' said my aunt, shortly."

"'She was very beautiful,' my grandmother gently recommenced. She said this, not precisely as an excuse, but with something of the sort in her tone. 'Very beautiful! How stately she did look that night, to be sure! She did not paint, and her complexion (a shade too high by day) was perfection by candlelight. I can see her now, my dear, as she stood up for a minuet with him. We wore hoops, then; and she had a white brocade petticoat, embroidered with pink rosebuds, and a train and bodice of pea-green satin, and green satin shoes with pink heels. You never saw anything more lovely than that brocade. A rich old aunt had given it to her. The shades of the rosebuds were exquisite. I embroidered the rosebuds on that salmon-coloured cushion downstairs from a piece that Anastatia gave me as a pattern. Dear me! What a dress it was, and how lovely she looked in it! Her eyes were black, a thing you rarely see, and they shone and glittered under her powdered hair. She had a delicately curved nose; splendid teeth, too, and showed them when she smiled. Then such a lovely throat, and beautifully-shaped arms! I don't know how it is, my dear Harriet,' added my grandmother, thoughtfully, 'but you don't see the splendid women now-a-days that there were when I was young. There are plenty of pretty, lively girls (rather too lively, in my old-fashioned judgment), but not the real stately beauty that it was worth a twenty miles' drive there and back, just to see, at one of the old county balls.'"

"My aunt sniffed, partly from a depressing consciousness of being one of a degenerate generation, and of a limited experience in the matter of county balls; partly also to express her conviction that principle is above beauty. She said:

"'Then Miss Eden married, ma'am?'"

"'Yes, rather late, Mr. Moss; a wealthy Indian merchant, I believe. She lost all her children, I know, one after another, and then he died. Poor Anastatia! It seems like yesterday. And to think she should be coming here!'"

"My grandmother sighed again, and I held my breath, hoping for some further particulars of the lovely heroine of this romance. But I was disappointed. My uncle's voice at this moment called loudly from below, and Aunt Harriet hurried off with a conscious meritoriousness about her, becoming a lady who had married the right man, and took great care of him.

"'Supper, ma'am. I think,' she said, as she left the room.

"My grandmother sat still by the fire, sighing gently now and then, and I lay making up my mind to brave all and tell her that I was awake. In the first place (although I was not intentionally eavesdropping, and my being awake was certainly not my fault), I felt rather uneasy at having overheard what I knew was not intended for my hearing. Besides this, I wanted to hear some more stories of the lovely Mrs. Moss, and to ask how soon she would come to the manor. After a few seconds my grandmother rose and toddled across the room. I made an effort, and spoke just above my breath:

"'Granny!'"

"But my grandmother was rather deaf. Moreover, my voice may have been drowned in the heavy sigh with which she closed the nursery door.

"The room was empty again; the glare of the red screen was tenderly subdued in the firelight; but for all this I did not go to sleep. I took advantage of my freedom to sit up in bed, toss my hair from my forehead, and clasping my knees with my arms, to rock myself and think. My thoughts had one object; my whole mind was filled with one image—Mrs. Moss. The future inhabitant of my dear deserted manor would, in any circumstances, have been an interesting subject for my fancies. The favoured individual whose daily walk might be between the yew-hedges on that elastic lawn; who should eat, drink, and sleep through the commonplace hours of this present time behind those mystical white shutters! But when the individual added to this felicitous dispensation of fortune the personal attributes of unparalleled beauty and pea-green satin; of having worn hoops, high heels, and powder; of countless lovers, and white brocade with pink rosebuds—well might I sit, my brain whirling with anticipation, as I thought: 'She is coming here: I shall see her!' For though, of course, I knew that having lived in those (so to speak) pre-historic times when my grandmother was young, Mrs. Moss must now be an old woman; yet, strange as it may seem, my dear, I do assure you that I never realized the fact. I thought of her as I had heard of her—young and beautiful—and modelled my hopes accordingly.

"Most people's day-dreams take, sooner or later, a selfish turn. I seemed to identify myself with the beautiful Anastatia. I thought of the ball as one looks back to the past. I fancied myself moving through the *minuet de la cour*, whose stately paces scarcely made the silken rosebuds rustle. I rejected *en masse* countless suitors of fabulous wealth and nobility; but when it came to Mr. Sandford, I could feel with Miss Eden no more. My grandmother had said that she loved him, that she encouraged him, and that she gave him up for money. It was a mystery! In her place, I thought, I would have danced every dance with him! I would have knitted for him in winter, and gathered flowers for him in the summer hedges. To whom should one be most kind, if not to those whom one most loves? To love, and take pleasure in giving pain—to balance a true heart and clear blue eyes against money, and prefer money—was not at that time comprehensible by me. I pondered, and (so to speak) spread out the subject before my mind, and sat in judgment upon it.

"Money—that is, golden guineas (my grandmother had given me one on my birthday), crowns, shillings, sixpences, pennies, halfpennies, farthings; and when you come to consider how many things a guinea judiciously expended in a toy-shop will procure, you see that money is a great thing, especially if you have the full control of it, and are not obliged to spend it on anything useful.

"On the other hand, those whom you love and who love you—not in childhood, thank God, the smallest part of one's acquaintance."

"I made a list on my own account. It began with my mother, and ended with my yellow cat. (It included a crusty old gardener, who was at times, especially in the spring, so particularly cross that I *might* have been tempted to exchange *him* for the undisputed possession of that stock of seeds, tools, and flower-pots which formed our chief subject of dispute. But this is a digression.) I took the lowest. Could I part with Sandy Tom for any money, or for anything that money could buy? I thought of a speaking doll, a miniature piano, a tiny carriage drawn by four yellow mastiffs, of a fairy purse that should never be empty, with all that might thereby be given to others or kept for oneself: and then I thought of Sandy Tom—of his large, round, soft head; his fine eyes (they were yellow, not blue, and glared with infinite tenderness); his melodious purr; his expressive whiskers; his incomparable tail.

"Love rose up as an impulse, an instinct; it would not be doubted, it utterly refused to be spread out to question."

"'Oh, Puss?' I thought, 'if you could but leap on to the bed at this moment I would explain it all to our mutual comprehension and satisfaction. My dear Sandy,' I would say, 'with you to lie on the cushioned seat, a nice little carriage, and four yellow mastiffs, would be perfection; but as to comparing what I love—to wit, you, Sandy!—with what I want—to wit, four yellow mastiffs and a great many other things besides—I should as soon think of cutting off your tail to dust the dolls' house with.' Alas! Sandy Tom was at home;

I could only imagine the gentle rub of the head with which he would have assented. Meanwhile, I made up my mind firmly on one point. My grandmother was wrong. Miss Anastatia Eden had not loved Mr. Sandford.

"Smash! The fire, which had been gradually becoming hollow, fell in at this moment, and I started to find myself chilly and cramped, and so lay down. Then my thoughts took another turn. I wondered if I should grow up beautiful, like Mrs. Moss. It was a serious question. I had often looked at myself in the glass, but I had a general idea that I looked much like other little girls of my age. I began gravely to examine myself in detail, beginning from the top of my head. My hair was light, and cropped on a level with the lobes of my ears; this, however, would amend itself with time; and I had long intended that my hair should be of raven blackness, and touch the ground at least; 'but that will not be till I am grown up,' thought I. Then my eyes: they were large; in fact, the undue proportions they assumed when I looked ill or tired formed a family joke. If size were all that one requires in eyes, mine would certainly pass muster. Moreover, they had long curly lashes. I fingered these slowly, and thought of Sandy's whiskers. At this point I nearly fell asleep, but roused myself to examine my nose. My grandmother had said that Mrs. Moss's nose was delicately curved. Now, it is certainly true that a curve may be either concave or convex; but I had heard of the bridge of a nose, and knew well enough which way the curve should go; and I had a shrewd suspicion that if so very short a nose as mine, with so much and so round a tip, could be said to be curved at all, the curve went the wrong way; at the same time I could not feel sure. For I must tell you that to lie in a comfortable bed, at an hour long beyond the time when one ought naturally to be asleep, and to stroke one's nose, is a proceeding not favourable to forming a clear judgment on so important a point as one's personal appearance. The very shadows were still as well as

Juliana Horatia Ewing

silent, the fire had ceased to flicker, a delicious quietude pervaded the room, as I stroked my nose and dozed, and dozed and stroked my nose, and lost all sense of its shape, and fancied it a huge lump growing under my fingers. The extreme unpleasantness of this idea just prevented my falling asleep; and I roused myself and sat up again.

"'It's no use feeling,' I thought, 'I'll look in the glass.'"

"There was one mirror in the room. It hung above the mantelpiece. It was old, deeply framed in dark wood, and was so hung as to slope forwards into the room.

"In front of the fire stood an old-fashioned, cushioned arm-chair, with a very high back, and a many-frilled chintz cover. A footstool lay near it. It was here that my grandmother had been sitting. I jumped out of bed, put the footstool into the chair that I might get to a level with the glass, and climbed on to it. Thanks to the slope of the mirror, I could now see my reflection as well as the dim firelight would permit.

"'What a silly child!' you will say, Ida. Very silly, indeed, my dear. And how one remembers one's follies! At the end of half a century, I recall my reflection in that old nursery mirror more clearly than I remember how I looked in the glass before which I put on my bonnet this evening to come to tea with you: the weird, startled glance of my eyes, which, in their most prominent stage of weariness, gazed at me out of the shadows of the looking glass, the tumbled tufts of hair, the ghostly effect of my white night-dress. As to my nose, I could absolutely see nothing of its shape; the firelight just caught the round tip, which shone like a little white toadstool from the gloom, and this was all.

"'One can't see the shape, full face,' I thought. 'If I had only another looking-glass.'"

"But there was not another. I knew it, and yet involuntarily looked round the room. Suddenly I exclaimed aloud, 'Mr. Joseph will do!'"

"Who was Mr. Joseph?—you will ask. My dear Ida, I really do not know. I have not the least idea. I had heard him called Mr. Joseph, and I fancy he was a connection of the family. All I knew of him was his portrait, a *silhouette*, elegantly glazed and framed in black wood, which hung against the nursery wall. I was ignorant of his surname and history. I had never examined his features. But I knew that happily he had been very stout, since his ample coat and waistcoat, cut out in black paper, converted the glass which covered them into an excellent mirror for my dolls.

"Worthy Mr. Joseph! Here he was coming in useful again. How much we owe to our forefathers! I soon unhooked him, and climbing back into the chair, commenced an examination of my profile by the process of double reflection. But all in vain! Whether owing to the dusty state of the mirror, or to the dim light, or to the unobliging shapeliness of Mr. Joseph's person, I cannot say, but, turn and twist as I would, I could not get a view of my profile sufficiently clear and complete to form a correct judgment upon. I held Mr. Joseph, now high, now low; I stooped, I stood on tiptoe, I moved forward, I leant backward. It was this latest manoeuvre that aggravated the natural topheaviness of the chair, and endangered its balance. The fore-legs rose, my spasmodic struggle was made in the wrong direction, and I, the arm-chair, and Mr. Joseph fell backwards together.

"Two of us were light enough, and happily escaped unhurt. It was the arm-chair which fell with such an appalling crash, and whether it were any the worse or no, I could not tell as it lay. As soon as I had a little recovered from the shock, therefore, I struggled to raise it, whilst Mr. Joseph lay

Juliana Horatia Ewing

helplessly upon the ground, with his waistcoat turned up to the ceiling.

"It was thus that my aunt found us.'

"If only Mr. Joseph and I had fallen together, no one need have been the wiser; but that lumbering arm-chair had come down with a bump that startled the sober trio at supper in the dining-room below.

"'What *is* the matter?' said Aunt Harriet."

"I was speechless."

"'What have you been doing?'"

"I couldn't speak; but accumulating misfortune was gradually overpowering me, and I began to cry."

"'Get into bed,' said Aunt Harriet."

"I willingly obeyed, and Aunt Harriet seated herself at the foot."

"'Now, think before you speak, Mary,' she said quietly, 'and then tell me the truth. What have you been doing?'"

"One large tear rolled over my nose and off the tip as I feebly began—

"'I got into the chair—'"

"'Well?' said Aunt Harriet."

"'—to look in the glass.'"

"'What for?' said Aunt Harriet."

"Tears flowed unrestrainedly over my face as I howled in self-abasement—

"'To look at the shape of my nose.'"

"At this point Aunt Harriet rose, and, turning her back rather abruptly, crossed the room, and picked up Mr. Joseph. (I have since had reason to believe that she was with difficulty concealing a fit of laughter.)

"'What have you had this picture down for?' she inquired, still with her back to me."

"'I couldn't see,' I sobbed, 'and I got Mr. Joseph to help me.'"

"My aunt made no reply, and, still carefully concealing her face, restored Mr. Joseph to his brass nail with great deliberation."

"There is nothing like full confession. I broke the silence."

"'Aunt Harriet, I was awake when you and Granny were here, and heard what you said.'"

"'You are a very silly, naughty child,' my aunt severely returned. 'Why don't you go to sleep when you are sent to bed?'"

"'I can't,' I sobbed, 'with talking and candles.'"

"'You've got the screen,' said Aunt Harriet; and I cannot tell why, but somehow I lacked courage to say that the red screen was the chief instrument of torture!"

"'Well, go to sleep now,' she concluded, 'and be thankful

you're not hurt. You might have killed yourself.'"

"Encouraged by the gracious manner in which she tucked me up, I took a short cut to the information which I had failed to attain through Mr. Joseph.

"'Aunt Harriet,' I said, 'do you think I shall ever be as beautiful as Mrs. Moss?'"

"'I'm ashamed of you,' said Aunt Harriet."

"I climbed no more into the treacherous arm-chair. I eschewed the mirror. I left Mr. Joseph in peace upon the wall. I took no further trouble about the future prospects of my nose. But night and day I thought of Mrs. Moss. I found the old cushion, and sat by it, gazing at the faded tints of the rosebuds, till I imagined the stiff brocade in all its beauty and freshness. I took a vigorous drawing fit; but it was only to fill my little book with innumerable sketches of Mrs. Moss. My uncle lent me his paint-box, as he was wont; and if the fancy portraits that I made were not satisfactory even to myself, they failed in spite of cheeks blushing with vermilion, in spite of eyes as large and brilliant as lamp-black could make them, and in spite of the most accurately curved noses that my pencil could produce. The amount of gamboge and Prussian blue that I wasted in vain efforts to produce a satisfactory pea-green, leaves me at this day an astonished admirer of my uncle's patience. At this time I wished to walk along no other road than that which led to my dear manor, where the iron gates were being painted, the garden made tidy, and the shutters opened; but, above all, the chief object of my desires was to accompany my grandmother and aunt in their first visit to Mrs. Moss.

"Once I petitioned Aunt Harriet on this subject. Her answer was—

"'My dear, there would be nothing to amuse you; Mrs. Moss is an old woman.'"

"'Granny said she was so beautiful,' I suggested."

"'So she was, my dear, when your grandmother was young.'"

"These and similar remarks I heard and heeded not. They did not add one wrinkle to my ideal of Mrs. Moss: they in no way whatever lessened my desire of seeing her. I had never seen my grandmother young, and her having ever been so seemed to me at the most a matter of tradition; on the other hand, Mrs. Moss had been presented to my imagination in the bloom of youth and beauty, and, say what they would, in the bloom of youth and beauty I expected to see her still.

"One afternoon, about a week after the arrival of Mrs. Moss, I was busy in the garden, where I had been working for an hour or more, when I heard carriage wheels drive up and stop at our door. Could it be Mrs. Moss? I stole gently round to a position where I could see without being seen, and discovered that the carriage was not that of any caller, but my uncle's. Then Granny and Aunt Harriet were going out. I rushed up to the coachman, and asked where they were going. He seemed in no way overpowered by having to reply—'To the manor, Miss.'"

"That was to Mrs. Moss, and I was to be left behind! I stood speechless in bitter disappointment, as my grandmother rustled out in her best silk dress, followed by Aunt Harriet and my uncle, who, when he saw me, exclaimed:

"'Why, there's my little Mary! Why don't you take her? I'll be bound she wants to go.'"

"'I do, indeed!' I exclaimed, in Cinderella-like tones."

"'But Mrs. Moss is such an old lady,' said Aunt Harriet, whose ideas upon children were purely theoretical, and who could imagine no interests for them apart from other children, from toys or definite amusements—'What could the child do with herself?'"

"'Do!' said my uncle, who took a rough and cheery view of life, 'why, look about her, to be sure. And if Mrs. M. is an old lady, there'll be all the more Indian cabinets and screens, and japanned tables, and knick-knacks, and lap-dogs. Keep your eyes open, Miss Mary. I've never seen the good lady or her belongings, but I'll stake my best hat on the japan ware and the lap-dog. Now, how soon can you be dressed?'"

"Later in life the selfish element mixes more largely with our admirations. A few years thence, and in a first interview with the object of so many fancies, I should have thought as much of my own appearance on the occasion, as of what I was myself to see. I should have taken some pains with my toilette. At that time, the desire to see Mrs. Moss was too absorbing to admit of any purely personal considerations. I dashed into the nursery, scrubbed my hands and face to a raw red complexion, brushed my hair in three strokes, and secured my things with one sweep. I hastily pocketed a pincushion of red cloth, worked with yellow silk spots, in the likeness of a strawberry. It was a pet treasure of mine, and I intended it as an offering to Mrs. Moss. I tied my hood at the top of the stairs, fastened my tippet in the hall, and reached the family coach by about three of those bounds common to all young animals.

"'Halloa!' said my uncle, with his face through the carriage door. 'You've not thanked me yet.'"

"I flung my arms round his starched neck-cloth."

"'You're a darling!' I exclaimed, with an emphatic squeeze."

"'You're another,' he replied, returning the embrace upon my hood."

"With this mutual understanding we parted, and I thought that if Mrs. Moss were not certain to fulfil my ideal, I should have wished her to be as nearly like Uncle James as the circumstances of the case would permit. I watched his yellow waistcoat and waving hands till they could be seen no longer, and then I settled myself primly upon the back seat, and ventured upon a shy conciliating promise to be 'very good.'"

"'You're quite welcome to come, child,' said Aunt Harriet; 'but as I said, there are neither children nor playthings for you.'"

"Children or playthings! What did I want with either? I put my arm through the loop by the window and watched the fields as they came and vanished, with vacant eyes, and thought of Mrs. Moss. A dozen times had I gone through the whole scene in my mind before we drove through the iron gates. I fancied myself in the bare, spacious hall, at which I had peeped; I seemed to hear a light laugh, and to see the beautiful face of Mrs. Moss look over the banisters; to hear a rustle, and the scraping of the stiff brocade, as the pink rosebuds shimmered, and the green satin shoes peeped out, and tap, tap, tap, the high pink heels resounded from the shallow stairs.

"I had dreamed this day-dream many times over before the carriage stopped with a shake, and Aunt Harriet roused me, asking if I were asleep. In another minute or so we were in the hall, and here I met with my first disappointment.

Juliana Horatia Ewing

"To begin with, I had seen the hall unfurnished, and had not imagined it otherwise. I had pictured Mrs. Moss in her beauty and rose brocade, the sole ornament of its cold emptiness. Then (though I knew that my grandmother and aunt must both be present) I had really fancied myself the chief character in this interview with Mrs. Moss. I had thought of myself as rushing up the stairs to meet her, and laying the pincushion at her green satin feet. And now that at last I was really in the hall, I should not have known it again. It was carpeted from end to end. Fragrant orange-trees stood in tubs, large hunting-pictures hung upon the walls, below which stood cases of stuffed birds, and over all presided a footman in livery, who himself looked like a stuffed specimen of the human race with unusually bright plumage.

"No face peeped over the banisters, and when we went upstairs, the footman went first (as seemed due to him), then my grandmother, followed by my aunt, and lastly I, in the humblest insignificance, behind them. My feet sank into the soft stair-carpets, I vacantly admired the elegant luxury around me, with an odd sensation of heartache. Everything was beautiful, but I had wanted nothing to be beautiful but Mrs. Moss.

"Already the vision began to fade. That full-fed footman troubled my fancies. His scarlet plush killed the tender tints of the rosebuds in my thoughts, and the streaky powder upon his hair seemed a mockery of the *toupee* I hoped to see, whose whiteness should enhance the lustre of rare black eyes. He opened the drawing-room door and announced my grandmother and aunt. I followed, and (so far as one may be said to face anything when one stands behind the skirts of two intervening elders) I was face to face with Mrs. Moss.

"That is, I was face to face with a tall, dark, old woman, with stooping shoulders, a hooked nose, black eyes that smouldered in their sunken sockets, and a distinct growth of beard upon her chin. Mr. Moss had been dead many years, and his widow had laid aside her weeds. She wore a dress of *feuille-morte* satin, and a black lace shawl. She had a rather elaborate cap, with a tendency to get on one side, perhaps because it would not fit comfortably on the brown front with bunchy curls which was fastened into its place by a band of broad black velvet.

"And this was Mrs. Moss! This was the end of all my fancies! There was nothing astonishing in the disappointment; the only marvel was that I should have indulged in so foolish a fancy for so long. I had been told more than once that Mrs. Moss was nearly as old as my grandmother. As it was, she looked older. Why—I could not tell then, though I know now.

"My grandmother, though never a beauty, had a sweet smile of her own, and a certain occasional kindling of the eyes, the outward signs of a character full of sentiment and intelligence; and these had outlasted youth. She had always been what is called 'pleasing,' and she was pleasing still. But in Mrs. Moss no strength, no sentiment, no intellect filled the place of the beauty that was gone. Features that were powerful without character, and eyes that glowed without expression, formed a wreck with little to recall the loveliness that had bewildered Mr. Sandford—and me.

"There is not much more to tell, Ida. This was the disappointment. This is the cause of my dislike for a certain shade of *feuille-morte* satin. It disappointed me of that rose brocade which I was never to see. You shall hear how I got through the visit, however. This meeting, which (like so many meetings) had proved the very reverse of what was hoped.

"Through an angle of Aunt Harriet's pelisse, I watched the meeting between my grandmother and Mrs. Moss. They

Juliana Horatia Ewing

kissed and then drew back and looked at each other, still holding hands. I wondered if my grandmother felt as I felt. I could not tell. With one of her smiles, she bent forward, and, kissing Mrs. Moss again, said:

"'God bless you, Anastatia.'"

"'God bless you, Elizabeth.'"

"It was the first time Mrs. Moss had spoken, and her voice was rather gruff. Then both ladies sat down, and my grandmother drew out her pocket-handkerchief and wiped her eyes. Mrs. Moss began (as I thought) to look for hers, and, not finding it, called,

"'Metcalfe!'"

on which a faded little woman, with a forefinger in a faded-looking book, came out from behind some window-curtains, and, rummaging Mrs. Moss's chair with a practised hand, produced a large silver snuff-box, from which Mrs. Moss took a pinch, and then offered it to Granny, who shook her head. Mrs. Moss took another and a larger pinch. It was evident what made her voice so gruff.

"Aunt Harriet was introduced as 'My daughter Harriet,' and made a stiff curtsey as Mrs. Moss smiled, and nodded, and bade her 'sit down, my dear.' Throughout the whole interview she seemed to be looked upon by both ladies as a child, and played the part so well, sitting prim and silent on her chair, that I could hardly help humming as I looked at her:

'Hold up your head,
Turn out your toes,
Speak when you're spoken to,
Mend your clothes.'

I was introduced, too, as 'a grandchild,' made a curtsey the shadow of Aunt Harriet's, received a nod, the shadow of that bestowed upon her, and got out of the way as soon as I could, behind my aunt's chair, where, coming unexpectedly upon three fat pug-dogs on a mat, I sat down among them and felt quite at home.

"The sight of the pugs brought Uncle James to my mind, and when I looked round the room, it seemed to me that he must be a conjuror at least, so true was everything he had said. A large Indian screen hid the door; japanned boxes stood on a little table to correspond in front of it, and there were two cabinets having shallow drawers with decorated handles, and a great deal of glass, through which odd teacups, green dragons, Indian gods, and Dresden shepherdesses were visible upon the shelves. The room was filled with knickknacks, and here were the pug-dogs, no less than three of them! They were very fat, and had little beauty except as to their round heads and black wrinkled snouts, which I kissed over and over again.

"'Do you mind Mrs. Moss's being old, and dressing in that hideous brown dress?' I asked in a whisper at the ear of one of these round heads. 'Think of the rosebuds on the brocade, and the pea-green satin, and the high-heeled shoes. Ah!' I added, 'you are only a pug, and pugs don't think.' Nevertheless, I pulled out the pincushion, and showed it to each dog in turn, and the sight of it so forcibly reminded me of my vain hopes, that I could not help crying. A hot tear fell upon the nose of the oldest and fattest pug, which so offended him that he moved away to another mat at some distance, and as both the others fell fast asleep, I took refuge in my own thoughts.

"The question arose why should not Mrs. Moss have the pincushion after all? I had expected her to be young and

Juliana Horatia Ewing

beautiful, and she had proved old and ugly, it is true; but there is no reason why old and ugly people should not have cushions to keep their pins in. It was a struggle to part with my dear strawberry pincushion in the circumstances, but I had fairly resolved to do so, when the rustle of leave-taking began, and I had to come out of my corner.

"'Bid Mrs. Moss good-day, Mary,' said my grandmother; and added, 'the child has been wild to come and see you, Anastatia.'"

"Mrs. Moss held out her hand good-naturedly. 'So you wanted to see me, my dear?' said she."

"I took my hand out of my pocket, where I had been holding the pincushion, and put both into Mrs. Moss's palm."

"'I brought this for you ma'am,' I said. 'It is not a real strawberry; it is emery; I made it myself.'"

"And the fact of having sacrificed something for Mrs. Moss made me almost fond of her. Moreover, there was an expression in her eyes at that moment which gave them beauty. She looked at my grandmother and laid her hand on my head.

"'I lost all mine, Elizabeth.'"

"I thought she was speaking of her pincushions, and being in a generous mood, said hastily,

"When that is worn out, ma'am, I will make you another.'"

"But she was speaking of her children. Poor Mrs. Moss! She took another huge pinch of snuff, and called, 'Metcalfe.'"

"The faded little woman appeared once more."

"'I must give you a keepsake in return, my dear,' said Mrs. Moss. 'The china pug, Metcalfe!'"

"Metcalfe (whose face always wore a smile that looked as if it were just about to disappear, and who, indeed, for that matter, always looked as if she were just about to disappear herself) opened one of the cabinets, and brought out a little toy pug in china, very delicately coloured, and looking just like one of my friends on the mat. I fell in love with it at once, and it was certainly a handsome exchange for the strawberry pincushion.

"'You will send the child to see me now and then, Elizabeth?' said Mrs. Moss as we retired."

"In the end Mrs. Moss and I became great friends. I put aside my dream among the 'vain fancies' of life, and took very kindly to the manor in its new aspect. Even the stuffed footman became familiar, and learnt to welcome me with a smile. The real Mrs. Moss was a more agreeable person than I have, I fear, represented her. She had failed to grasp solid happiness in life, because she had chosen with the cowardice of an inferior mind; but she had borne disappointment with dignity, and submitted to heavy sorrows with patience; and a greater nature could not have done more. She was the soul of good humour, and the love of small chat, which contrasted so oddly with her fierce appearance, was a fund of entertainment for me, as I fed my imagination and stored my memory with anecdotes of the good old times in the many quiet evenings we spent together. I learnt to love her more heartily, I confess, when she bought a new gown and gave the *feuille-morte* satin to Mrs. Metcalfe.

"Mrs. Metcalfe was 'humble companion' to Mrs. Moss. She

Juliana Horatia Ewing

was in reality single, but she exacted the married title as a point of respect. At the beginning of our acquaintance I called her 'Miss Metcalfe,' and this occasioned the only check our friendship ever received. Now I would, with the greatest pleasure, have addressed her as 'My Lord Archbishop,' or in any other style to which she was not entitled, it being a matter of profound indifference to me. But the question was a serious one to her, and very serious she made it, till I almost despaired of our ever coming to an understanding on the subject.

"On every other point she was unassuming almost to non-entity. She was weak-minded to the verge of mental palsy. She was more benevolent in deed, and more wandering in conversation, than any one I have met with since. That is, in ordinary life. In the greenhouse or garden (with which she and the head-gardener alone had any real acquaintance) her accurate and profound knowledge would put to shame many professed garden botanists I have met with since. From her I learnt what little I know of the science of horticulture, and with her I spent many happy hours over the fine botanical works in the manor library, which she alone ever opened.

"And so I became reconciled to things as they were, though to this day I connect with that shade of *feuille-morte* satin a disappointment not to be forgotten."

* * * * *

"It is a dull story, is it not, Ida?" said the little old lady, pausing here. She had not told it in precisely these words, but this was the sum and substance of it.

Ida nodded. Not that she had thought the story dull, so far as she had heard it, and whilst she was awake; but she had fallen asleep, and so she nodded.

Mrs. Overtheway looked back at the fire, to which, indeed, she had been talking for some time past.

"A child's story?" she thought. "A tale of the blind, wilful folly of childhood? Ah, my soul! Alas, my grown-up friends! Does the moral belong to childhood alone? Have manhood and womanhood no passionate, foolish longings, for which we blind ourselves to obvious truth, and of which the vanity does not lessen the disappointment? Do we not still toil after rosebuds, to find *feuilles-mortes*?"

No voice answered Mrs. Overtheway's fanciful questions. The hyacinth nodded fragrantly on its stalk, and Ida nodded in her chair. She was fast asleep—happily asleep—with a smile upon her face.

The shadows nodded gently on the walls, and like a shadow the little old lady stole quietly away.

When Ida awoke, she found herself lying partly in the arm-chair, and partly in the arms of Nurse, who was lifting her up. A candle flared upon the table, by the fire stood an empty chair, and the heavy scent that filled the room was as sweet as the remembrance of past happiness. The little old lady had vanished, and, but for the hyacinth, Ida would almost have doubted whether her visit had not been a dream.

"Has Mrs. Overtheway been long gone, Nursey?" she asked, keeping her eyes upon the flowerpot.

"Ever so long!" said Nurse, "and here you've been snoring away, and the old lady's been downstairs, telling me how comfortably you were asleep, and she's coming again to-morrow evening, if you're good."

It was precisely twelve minutes since Mrs. Overtheway left

the house, but Nurse was of a slightly exaggerative turn of mind, and few people speak exactly on the subject of time, especially when there is an opportunity of triumphing over someone who has been asleep before bed-time. The condition of Ida's being good was also the work of Nurse's own instructive fancy, but Ida caught eagerly at the welcome news of another visit.

"Then she is not angry with me for falling asleep, Nursey? I was so comfortable, and she has such a nice voice, I couldn't help it; I think I left off about the pugs. I wish I had a pug with a wrinkled black snout, don't you, Nursey?"

"I'm sure I don't, Miss Ida. My father kept all sorts of pigs, and we used to have one with a black snout and black spots, but it was as ugly as ugly could be; and I never could fancy the bacon would be fit to eat. You must have been dreaming, I'm sure; the old lady would never tell you about such rubbish, I know."

"It's pugs, not pigs, Nursey; and they're dogs, you know," said Ida, laughing. "How funny you are! And indeed she did tell me, I couldn't have dreamt it; I never dreamt anything so nice in my life."

"And never will, most likely," said Nurse, who was very skilful in concluding a subject which she did not want to discuss, and who was apt to do so by a rapid twist in the line of argument, which Ida would find somewhat bewildering. "But, dear Miss Ida," she continued, "do leave off clutching at that chair-arm, when I'm lifting you up; and your eyes 'll drop out of your head, if you go on staring like that."

Ida relaxed the nervous grasp, to which she had been impelled by her energy on the subject of the pugs, let down her eyebrows, and submitted to be undressed. The least pleasant part of this ceremony may be comprised in the word curl-papers. Ida's hair was dark, and soft, and smooth, but other little girls wore ringlets, and so this little girl must wear ringlets too. To that end her hair was every night put into curl-papers, with much tight twisting and sharp jerking, and Ida slept upon an irregular layer of small paper parcels, which made pillows a mockery. With all this, however, a damp day, or a good romp, would sometimes undo the night's work, to the great disgust of Nurse. In her last place, the young lady's hair had curled with a damp brush, as Ida well knew, and Nurse made so much of her own grievance, in having to use the curl-papers, that no place was left for Ida's grievance in having to sleep upon them. She submitted this night therefore, as other nights, in patience, and sat swinging her feet and accommodating her head to the sharp tugs, which always seemed to come from unexpected quarters. Perhaps, however, her mind may have been running a little upon grievances, which made her say:

"You know, Nursey, how you are always telling me I ought to be thankful for having things, and not having things, and—"

"I wish you'd talk sense, and not give way with your head so when I pull, Miss Ida," retorted Nurse, "having things, and not having things; I don't know what you mean."

"Well, you know, Nursey, the other day when I said I didn't like bread-and-treacle treacled so long before, and soaked in, and you said I ought to be thankful that I had bread-and-treacle at all, and that I hadn't a wooden leg, and to eat anything I could get, like the old sailor man at the corner; well, do you know, I've thought of something I *am* so thankful for, and that is that I haven't a red screen to my bed."

"I really do think, Miss Ida," said Nurse, "that you'll go out

Juliana Horatia Ewing

of your mind some day, with your outlandish fancies. And where you get them, I can't think. I'm sure *I* never put such things into your head."

Ida laughed again.

"Never mind, Nursey, it all belongs to the pug story. Am I done now? And when you've tucked me up, please, would you mind remembering to put the flower where I can see it when I wake?"

Nurse did as she was asked, and Ida watched the hyacinth till she fell asleep; and she slept well.

In the morning she took her old post at the window. The little old lady had never seemed so long in making her appearance, nor the bells so slow to begin. Chim! chime! chim! chime! There they were at last, and there was Mrs. Overtheway. She looked up, waved a bunch of snowdrops, and went after the bells. Ida kissed her hand, and waved it over and over again, long after the little old lady was out of sight.

"There's a kiss for you, dear Mrs. Overtheway," she cried, "and kisses for your flowers, and your house, and everything belonging to you, and for the bells and the church, and everybody in it this morning, and—"

But, at this point of universal benevolence, Nurse carried her off to breakfast.

The little old lady came to tea as before. She looked as well as ever, and Nurse was equally generous in the matter of tea and toast. Mrs. Overtheway told over again what Ida had missed in the story of Mrs. Moss, and Ida apologized, with earnest distress, for her uncivil conduct in falling asleep.

"There I was snoring away, when you were telling me such a delightful story!" she exclaimed, penitently.

"Not snoring exactly, my dear," smiled the little old lady, "but you looked very happy."

"I thought Nursey said so," said Ida. "Well, I'm very glad. It would have been too rude. And you know I don't know how it was, for I *am* so fond of stories; I like nothing so well."

"Well, shall I try again?" said Mrs. Overtheway. "Perhaps I may find a more amusing one, and if it does put you to sleep, it won't do any harm. Indeed, I think the doctor will say I'm very good company for you."

"You are very good! That *I* can tell him," said Ida, fervently, "and please let it be about yourself again, if you can remember anything. I like true stories."

"Talking of snoring," said Mrs. Overtheway, "reminds me of something that happened in my youth, and it is true, though, do you know, it is a ghost story."

Ida danced in her chair.

"That is just what I should like!" she exclaimed. "Nurse has a ghost story, belonging to a farm-house, which she tells the housemaid, but she says she can't tell me till I am older, and I should so like to hear a ghost story, if it isn't too horrid."

"This ghost story isn't too horrid, I think," laughed the little old lady, "and if you will let me think a few minutes, and then forgive my prosy way of telling it, you shall have it at once."

There was a pause. The little old lady sat silent, and so sat

Ida also, with her eyes intently fixed on Mrs. Overtheway's face, over which an occasional smile was passing.

"It's about a ghost who snored," said the little old lady, doubtfully.

"Delicious!" responded Ida. The two friends settled themselves comfortably, and in some such words as these was told the following story:—

THE SNORING GHOST

Clown. Madman, thou errest: I say there is no darkness but Ignorance, in which thou art more puzzled than the Egyptians in their fog.... What is the opinion of Pythagoras concerning wild fowl?

Malvolio. That the soul of our grandam might haply inhabit a bird.

Clown. What thinkest thou of his opinion?

Malvolio. I think nobly of the soul, and in no way approve his opinion.

—TWELFTH NIGHT, IV. 2.

"I remember," said Mrs. Overtheway, "I remember my first visit. That is, I remember the occasion when I and my sister Fatima did, for the first time in our lives, go out visiting without our mother, or any grown-up person to take care of us."

"Do you remember your mother?" asked Ida.

"Quite well, my dear, I am thankful to say. The best and kindest of mothers!"

"Was your father alive, too?" Ida asked, with a sigh.

The old lady paused, pitying the anxious little face opposite, but Ida went on eagerly:

"Please tell me what *he* was like."

"He was a good deal older than my mother, who had married very early. He was a very learned man. His tastes and accomplishments were many and various, and he was very young-hearted and enthusiastic in the pursuit of them all his life. He was apt to take up one subject of interest after another, and to be for the time completely absorbed in it. And, I must tell you, that whatever the subject might be, so long as his head was full of it, the house seemed full of it too. It influenced the conversation at meals, the habits of the household, the names of the pet animals, and even of the children. I was called Mary, in a fever of chivalrous enthusiasm for the fair and luckless Queen of Scotland, and Fatima received her name when the study of Arabic had brought about an eastern mania. My father had wished to call her Shahrazad, after the renowned sultana of the 'Arabian Nights' but when he called upon the curate to arrange for the baptism, that worthy man flatly rebelled. A long discussion ended in my father's making a list of eastern names, from which the curate selected that of Fatima as being least repugnant to the sobriety of the parish registers. So Fatima she was called, and as she grew up pale, and moon-faced, and dark-eyed, the name became her very well."

"Was it this Fatima who went out visiting with you?" asked Ida.

"Yes, my dear; and now as to the visit. The invitation came on my thirteenth birthday.

"One's birthday is generally a day of some importance. A very notable day whilst one is young, but less so when one is old, when one is being carried quickly through the last stages of life, and when it seems hardly worth while to count time so near the end of the journey. Even in youth, however some birthdays are more important than others. I remember looking forward to my tenth birthday as to a high point of dignity and advancement; and the just pride of the occasion on which I first wrote my age with more figures than one. With similar feelings, I longed to be thirteen. The being able to write my age with two figures had not, after all, shed any special lustre upon life; but when I was 'in my teens' it must 'feel different somehow.' So I thought. Moreover, this birthday was really to bring with it solid advantages. I was now to be allowed to read certain books of a more grown-up character than I had read hitherto, and to sit up till nine o'clock. I was to wear sandals to my shoes. My hair was henceforth to grow as long as I and the Fates would permit, and the skirts of my frocks were to take an inch in the same direction. 'In four more years,' I said to Fatima, as we sat on the eve of my birthday, discussing its manifold advantages, 'in four more years I shall be grown up. Miss Ansted was introduced at seventeen.' The prospect was illimitable.

"'Do people always grow much on their birthdays?' asked one of the little ones. I had boasted in the nursery, that when I was thirteen I should be 'nearly grown up,' and I myself had hardly outlived the idea that on one's birthday one was a year older than on the previous day, and might naturally expect to have made a year's growth during the night.

"This birthday, however, produced no such striking change. As usual, the presents were charming; the wreath as lovely as Fatima's deft fingers could make it, the general holiday and pleasure-making almost too much of a good thing. Otherwise, there was little to mark it from other days in the year.

"Towards evening we were all sitting on the grass, the boys with their heads on the sisters' laps, and there had been an outcry for a story, to which no one had responded; partly, perhaps, because the exquisite air of evening seemed a sufficient delight, the stillness too profound to be lightly disturbed. We had remained for some time without speaking, and the idea was becoming general among the girls that the boys were napping, when the summer silence was broken by the distant footfalls of a horse upon the high road.

"'Trotting!' observed one of the supposed sleepers. We were not, as a family, given to explanations, and we drew a few more breaths of the evening air in silence. Then someone said:

"'We might make a story out of *that*, and fancy all sorts of things. Who is it? Where does he come from, and where is he going to?'"

"'It is a messenger from the seat of war,' drawled the boy in my lap, without moving. Then, lifting his curly head for a moment, he cried, 'To horse! gentlemen, to horse! The enemy will be at Carter's Mill by midnight!'"

"There was a pause; the solitary footfalls came nearer through the evening mists, and a small brother, of a quaint turn of mind, much given to the study of the historical portions of the Old Testament, sat up and said, slowly:

"'It is one of Job's messengers. *The Chaldeans made out three bands, and fell upon the camels, and have carried them away, yea, and slain the servants with the edge of the sword; and I only am escaped alone to tell thee.*'"

"The others boys laughed, but he lay down again, as solemnly as he had risen."

"'That was a foot-messenger,' said my boy, contemptuously."

"'It doesn't say so,' retorted the small brother."

"'Well, any way, the camels had been carried off—so what did he ride upon?'"

"A squabble was imminent. I covered my boy's face with a handkerchief, to keep him quiet.

"'Listen!' I said. 'It's the post. The mail from the north was stopped on the highway, but he has saved the bags, and is riding hard for London.'"

"'It's—'"

"But the new suggestion was drowned in a general shout of—"

"'It's coming up the lane!'"

"The footfalls had diverged from the main road, and were coming up the sandy lane that skirted our wall. The boys lifted their heads, and we sat expectant. There was a pause, and a familiar gate-click, and then the footfalls broke upon the carriage-road, close by us. A man in livery, upon a well-groomed horse—nothing more, but rather an uncommon sight with us. Moreover, the man and his livery were strange, and the horse looked tired.

"This event broke up the sitting, and we were strolling up to the house, when a maid met us, saying that my mother wished to see me and Fatima.

"We found my mother sewing, with an opened letter beside her. It was written on one of the large quarto sheets then in use, and it was covered and crossed, at every available corner, in a vague, scratchy hand.

"'I have heard from an old friend of mine, Mary,' said my mother. 'She has come to live about twelves miles from here. There is something in the letter about you and Fatima, and you may read that part aloud, if you can. The top of the last page.'"

"I found the place, and, with some difficulty, deciphered: 'The dear Major was all delicacy and consideration—'"

"'No, no!' said my mother, 'the next sentence.'"

"'Dear Cecilia was all sweetness. The dress was—'"

"My mother took the letter, and found the right place herself, and then I read:

"'If you cannot come yourself, at least let us renew acquaintance in our children. I think you have two girls about thirteen? My Lucy, a dear child just fifteen, feels keenly the loss of her only sister, and some young companions would be a boon, as all our company will be *elders*. Pray send them. They can come by the coach, and shall be met at Durnford, at the Elephant and Castle.'"

"'Is the other sister dead?' asked Fatima, pityingly, when we had discussed our personal interest in the subject."

"'Oh, no! only married,' said my mother."

"It was decided that we should go. This decision was not arrived at at once, or without some ups and downs. My mother could not go herself, and had some doubts as to our being old enough, as yet, to go out visiting alone. It will be believed that I made much of being able to say—'But you know, I am thirteen, now.'"

"Next day, in the evening, my father was busy in his study, and my mother sat at the open window, with Fatima and me at her feet. The letter of acceptance had been duly sent by the messenger, but she had yet a good deal of advice to give, and some doubts to express. She was one of those people who cannot sit with idle fingers, and as she talked she knitted. We found it easy enough to sit idle upon two little footstools, listening to the dear kind voice, and watching two little clouds, fragments of a larger group, which had detached themselves, and were sailing slowly and alone across the heavens.

"'They are like us two,' Fatima had whispered to me; 'perhaps they are going to see some other clouds.'"

"'I have observed two things which are apt to befall young people who go out visiting,' said my mother, as she turned a row in her knitting, 'one is, that they neglect little good habits while they are away, and the other is, that they make themselves very disagreeable when they come back.'"

"The clouds drifted on, and my mother continued her knitting, arming us with many wise counsels on small matters connected with this great event; to which Fatima and I gratefully gave half our minds, whilst with the other half we made rosy pictures of unparalleled excellence under trying circumstances, by which, hereafter, we should prove these warnings and counsels to have been, in our case, unnecessary and superfluous.

"'Most families and most people,' said my mother, 'have little good habits and customs of their own which they feel bound to keep, although they are not among the great general duties which bind every one. So long as young people are at home, these matters are often simple enough, but when they go away certain difficulties arise. They go amongst people whose little habits are not the same as those to which they have been accustomed. Sometimes they come to very uncharitable conclusions upon their friends' characters in consequence. And, I must say, that I have never met with any one who could be more severe than young people of your age are apt to be. I remember it of myself, and I have seen it in so many other girls. Home is naturally the standard, and whatever is different seems wrong. As life goes on, these young critics learn (or should learn) to distinguish between general and particular duties; and also coming to know a larger number of people, they find that all good persons are not cut to the same pattern, and that one's friends' little ways are not therefore absurd, because one does not happen to be used to them. On the other hand, if going amongst other people may tempt you to be critical of their little habits, it is also apt to make you neglect your own. Perhaps you think this cannot much matter, as they are not the great duties, and as other people seem to get on quite well without them. But one learns in the end, that no character of any value is formed without the discipline of individual rules, and that rules are of no use that are not held to against circumstances. "Charitable to others, severe to himself," seems a maxim for grown-up people in grown-up things; but, I believe, my little daughters, that the doubts and difficulties of life begin very early, earlier than they are commonly provided against; I think that innumerable girls struggle miserably in the practice of duty, from a radical ignorance of its principles, and that the earlier these are learnt, the smaller is the burden of regret one heaps together to oppress the future, and the sooner one finds that peace of mind which is not common even amongst the young, and should-be light-hearted.'"

"In these, or words to this effect, my dear mother prepared us for our first plunge into society. We discussed the little good habits we were to maintain, and, amongst others, certain little Sunday customs—for we were to be away for a week.

"'We can't take all our good habits with us, if you won't come,' I said. 'What is to become of the Sunday readings?'"

"For my mother used to read to us every Sunday evening, and we were just in the middle of that book of wondrous fascination—'The Pilgrim's Progress.'"

"'If it were not for the others, and if you would trust us with it,' said Fatima, thoughtfully, 'we might take the book with us, and Mary might read to me, if she would—I like her reading.'"

"My mother consented. There was another copy in the house, and though this volume was a favourite, she said it was time we learnt to take care of valuable books. So it was settled. We talked no more that evening; and the clouds drifted out of sight.

"'They have gone to bed in a big dark cloud on the other side' said Fatima, yawning; and we went to bed also."

"My story wanders, Ida; this is because it is an old woman's tale. Old people of my age become prosy, my dear. They love to linger over little remembrances of youth, and to recall the good counsels of kind voices long silent. But I must not put you to sleep a second time, so I will not describe the lists of good habits which Fatima and I drew up in fine Roman characters, and which were to be kept as good resolutions had never been kept before. We borrowed the red ink, to make them the more impressive to the eye, and, unfortunately, spilt it. A bad beginning, as many of our rules had reference to tidiness. Neither will I give you the full account of how we packed. How our preparations began at once, and were only stopped by the necessity of setting off when the day arrived. How we emptied all our drawers and cupboards, and disarranged both our bookshelves; and, in making ready for the life of order and tidiness we were to live abroad, passed that week at home with our room in such chaos as it had never been before. How we prepared against an amount of spare time, that experience eventually teaches one is not to be found out visiting; and, with this object, took more sewing than we should have performed in a month at home; books, that we had not touched for years; drawings, that were fated to be once touched, and no more.

"I will not describe the big box, which my father lent to us, nor the joys of packing it. How Fatima's workbox dovetailed with my desk. How the books (not having been chosen with reference to this great event) were of awkward sizes, and did not make comfortable paving for the bottom of the trunk; whilst folded stockings may be called the packer's delight, from their usefulness to fill up corners. How, having packed the whole week long, we were barely ready, and a good deal flurried at the last moment; and how we took all our available property with us, and left the key of the trunk behind. Fancy for yourself, how the green coach picked us up at the toll-bar, and how, as it jingled on, we felt the first qualm of home-sickness, and, stretching our heads and hands out of the window, waved adieux and kisses innumerable to Home, regardless of our fellow-traveller in the corner, an old gentleman, with a yellow silk handkerchief on his head, who proved in the end a very pleasant companion. I remember that we told him our family history, with minutest particulars, and conjugated four regular Latin verbs by his orders; and that he rewarded our confidences and learning with the most clear, the most sweet, the most amber-coloured sticks of barley-sugar I have ever had the good fortune to meet with. I remember also how, in the warmth of our new friendship, Fatima unveiled to him the future, which, through some joke of my father's, we had laid out for ourselves.

"I am to marry a Sultan, for I am moon-faced; but Mary is to be a linguist, for she has large eyes.'"

"'Then Miss Mary is not to marry?' said the old gentleman, with a grim smile."

"I shook my head in sage disdain. 'When I am sixteen, I shall be an Amazon.'"

"Precisely what I meant by this I don't think I knew myself, but my dreams were an odd compound of heroic and fairy lore, with a love and ambition for learning that were simply an inheritance. Many a night did I fancy myself master of all the languages of the world, hunting up and down the windy hills in a dress of Lincoln green. I had a mighty contempt for men, and a high respect for myself, that was the greatest of my many follies.

"After these interesting revelations we had barley-sugar all round, and the coach rattled into Durnford."

"Shall I tell you how we were met at the Elephant and Castle by a footman of most gentlemanlike appearance (his livery excepted), who, with a sagacity which somewhat puzzled us, discovered that we were 'the young ladies that were expected,' and led us to the carriage, firmly opposing my efforts to fulfil the last home orders I had received, to 'look after the box?' How in the carriage we found a lady handsomely dressed in black, who came out to meet us, and seemed so anxious for our comfort, and so much interested in our arrival, that we naturally supposed her to be the lady who had invited us, till we discovered that she was a lady's maid; and on arriving found our hostess quite another sort of

Juliana Horatia Ewing

person, with no appearance at all of being particularly interested in our arrival, which I have since found to be the case with the heads of some other country houses.

"It was a large house, reminding me of the Manor within, but prettier outside; old and irregularly built, with mullioned windows, and odd wings and corners. A glowing, well-kept garden contrasted prettily with the grey stone, and the grounds seemed magnificent to our eyes.

"We were shown into the drawing-room, where the real lady of the house sat at a dainty writing-table, scratching away at a letter that was no doubt as affectionate as the one which my mother had received. She was shortsighted, which seemed to be the case also with most of the other ladies in the room; this, perhaps, was why they stared so hard at us, and then went on with the elaborate pieces of needlework on which all of them were engaged. It seemed to take our hostess a second or two to see us, and another second or two to recall who we were; then she came forward very kindly, showed us where to sit, and asked after my mother. Whilst I was replying, she crossed to the fire-place, and rang the bell; and I felt slightly surprised by her seeming to wish for no further news of her old friend. She asked if we had had a pleasant journey, and Fatima had hardly pronounced a modest yes, before she begged we would allow her to finish her letter, and went back to the spindle-legged table. Whilst she scratched we looked around us. Three or four ladies were in the room, more or less young, more or less pretty, more or less elegantly dressed, and all with more or less elaborate pieces of needlework. There was one gentleman, young and dark, with large brown eyes, who seemed to be employed in making paper pellets of an old letter, chatting the while in a low voice to a young lady with a good deal of red hair. We afterwards found out that he was an Irishman, familiarly called 'Pat' by some of the young ladies, who seemed to be related to him. We had seen all this when the man-servant appeared at the door.

"'Where is Miss Lucy, Thompson?' our hostess asked, sharply."

"'I will inquire, ma'am,' Thompson replied, with the utmost softness, and vanished."

"The scratching began again, the Irishman went on gently chatting, and it all felt very like a horrid dream. Then Thompson reappeared.

"'Miss Lucy is out, ma'am.'"

"'Did she know what time these young ladies were to arrive?'"

"'Miss Lucy knew that the carriage had gone to meet them, ma'am.'"

"'Very thoughtless! Very thoughtless indeed!' said the lady. Thompson paused respectfully, as if to receive the full weight of the remark, and then vanished noiselessly as before.

"There was an awkward pause. Our hostess left off scratching, and looked very cross; the Irishman fired one of his pellets across the room, and left off chatting, and the red-haired young lady got up, and rustled across to us. I remember her so well, Ida, for we fell deeply in love with her and her kindness. I remember her green and white dress. She had a fair round face, more pleasant than really pretty, a white starlike forehead, almost too firm a mouth, but a very gentle voice, at least, so we thought, when she said:

"'As Lucy is out, may I take these young ladies to their room?'"

Juliana Horatia Ewing

"Our hostess hesitated, and murmured something about Bedford, who was the lady's maid. The starlike forehead contracted, and the red-haired young lady said, rather emphatically:

"'As Lucy is not in to receive her friends, I thought I might perhaps supply her place.'"

"'Well, my dear Kate, if you will be so kind,' said our hostess, 'I must finish these letters.'"

"'The yellow room?' said the young lady, abruptly, and swept us off without further parley. The Irish gentleman opened the door for us, staring with a half-puzzled, half-amused look at the lofty air with which the young lady passed out. He followed us into the hall, where we left him discharging his remaining pellets at the furniture, and whistling 'Kathleen Mavourneen,' as clearly as a bird.

"The yellow room was a large airy one, with white painted wainscoting, a huge four-post bed with yellow curtains, and a pretty view from the windows. In the middle of the floor we saw our box standing in all its dignity, uncorded, and ready. Then it was the terrible fact broke upon our minds that the key was left behind. My sufferings during the few seconds before I found courage to confide this misfortune to our new friend were considerable. When I did tell her, the calmness and good nature with which she received the confession were both surprising and delightful.

"'The lock doesn't look a very uncommon one, she said, as she opened the door. 'I dare say I may find a key to fit it.'"

"'What's the matter?' said a voice outside. It was the Irish gentleman. She explained.

"'Keys?' said the Irish gentleman; 'got lots in my pocket, besides their being totally unnecessary, as I'm a capital hand at lock-picking. Let me see.'"

"With which he slipped in, seeming quite as much at his ease as in the drawing-room, and in another second had squatted upon the floor before our box, where he seemed to be quite as comfortable as in the arm-chair he had left. Here he poked, and fitted, and whistled, and chatted without a pause.

"'I've locks and keys to everything I possess' he cheerfully remarked; 'and as I never lock up anything, there's no damage done if the keys are left behind, which is a good thing, you see, as I always leave everything everywhere.'"

"'Do you make a principle of it?' asked the young lady, coldly."

"'I'm afraid I make a practice of it.' He had opened the box, and was leaning against the bed-post, with a roguish twinkle in his brown eyes, which faded, however, under the silent severity of the red-haired young lady, and gave place to a look of melancholy that might have melted granite, as he added:

"'I'm all alone, you see, that's what does it. I believe I'm the neatest creature breathing, if I'd only somebody to keep me up to it.'"

"Neither his hardened untidiness nor his lonely lot seemed, however, to weigh heavily on his mind; for he withdrew whistling, and his notes were heard about the passages for some little time. When they had died away in a distant part of the house, the red-haired young lady left us also.

"I shall not give you a lengthened account of our unpacking, dear Ida; though it was as enjoyable, but less protracted than the packing-up had been. How we revelled in the spacious drawers and cupboards, over which we were queens, and how strictly we followed one of our mother's wise counsels—'unpack to the bottom of your box at once, however short your visit may be; it saves time in the end.' We did unpack to the lowest book (an artificial system of memory, which I had long been purposing to study, which I thought to find spare moments to get up here, and which, I may as well confess, I did not look at during the visit, and have not learnt to this day). We divided shelves and pegs with all fairness, and as a final triumph found a use for the elaborate watch-pockets that hung above our pillows. They were rich with an unlimited expenditure of quilled ribbon, and must have given a great deal of trouble to someone who had not very many serious occupations in this life. Fatima and I wished that we had watches to put in them, till the happy thought suddenly struck one of us, that we could keep in them our respective papers of good habits.

"Bedford came in whilst we were in the midst of our labours, and warmly begged us to leave everything to her, as she would put our things away for us. The red-haired young lady had sent her, and she became a mainstay of practical comfort to us during our visit. She seemed a haven of humanity after the conventions of the drawing-room. From her we got incidental meals when we were hungry, spirits of wine when Fatima's tooth ached, warnings when we were near to being late for breakfast, little modern and fashionable turns to our hair and clothes, and familiar anecdotes of this household and of others in which she had lived. I remember her with gratitude.

"Miss Lucy came home before our putting away was fairly finished, and we had tea with her in the schoolroom. She was a slight, sharp, lively young lady, looking older than fifteen to us, rather pretty, and very self-possessed. She scanned us from head to foot when we first met, and I felt as if her eyes had found defects innumerable, which seemed the less likely, as she also was shortsighted. As her governess was away visiting a sick relative, Miss Lucy did the honours of the schoolroom. She was cold and inattentive at first, became patronizing at tea, and ended by being gracious. In her gracious mood she was both affectionate and confidential. She called us 'my dear girls,' put her arms round us as we sat in the dark, and chattered without a pause about herself, her governesses, her sister, and her sister's husband.

"'A wedding in the house,' she observed, 'is very good fun, particularly if you take a principal part in it. I was chief bride's-maid, you know, my dear girls. But I'll tell you the whole affair from the first. You know I had never been bride's-maid before, and I couldn't make up my mind about how I should like the dresses,' etc., etc. And we had got no further in the story than Miss Lucy's own costume, when we were called to dress and go downstairs.

"'What are you going to put on?' she asked, balancing herself at our door and peering in."

"'White muslin!' we said with some pride, for they were new frocks, and splendid in our eyes."

"'I have had so many muslins, I am tired of them,' she said; 'I shall wear a pink silk to-night. The trimming came from London. Perhaps I may wear a muslin to-morrow; I have an Indian one. But you shall see my dresses to-morrow, my dear girls.'"

"With which she left us, and we put on our new frocks (which were to be *the* evening dresses of our visit) in depressed spirits. This was owing to the thought of the pink

Juliana Horatia Ewing

silk, and of the possibility of a surfeit of white muslin.

"During the evening we learnt another of Miss Lucy's peculiarities. Affectionate as she had been when we were alone together, she was no sooner among the grown-up young ladies downstairs than she kept with them as much as she was permitted, and seemed to forget us altogether. Perhaps a fit of particularly short sight attacked her; for she seemed to look over us, away from us, on each side of us, anywhere but at us, and to be quite unconscious of our existence. The red-haired young lady had made her fetch us a large scrap-book, and we sat with this before our eyes, and the soft monotonous chit-chat of our hostess in our ears, as she talked and worked with some elder ladies on the sofa. It seemed a long gossip, with no particular end or beginning, in which tatting, trimmings, military distinction, linens, servants, honourable conduct, sentiment, settlements, expectations, and Bath waters, were finely blended. From the constant mention of Cecilia and the dear major, it was evident that the late wedding was the subject of discourse; indeed, for that matter, it remained the prime topic of conversation during our stay.

"Cecilia and the dear major were at Bath, and their letters were read aloud at the breakfast-table. I remember wondering at the deep interest that all the ladies seemed to take in the bride's pretty flow of words about the fashions, the drives, and the pump-room, and the long lists of visitors' names; this, too, without any connection between the hearers and the people and places mentioned. When anybody did recognize a name, however, about which she knew anything, it seemed like the finding of a treasure. All the ladies bore down upon it at once, dug up the family history to its farthest known point, and divided the subject among them. Miss Lucy followed these letters closely, and remembered them wonderfully, though (as I afterwards found) she had never seen Bath, and knew no more of the people mentioned than the little hearsay facts she had gathered from former letters.

"It is a very useful art, my dear Ida, and one in which I have sadly failed all my life, to be able to remember who is related to whom, what watering-place such a family went to the summer before last, and which common friends they met there, etc. But, like other arts, it demands close attention, forbids day-dreaming, and takes up a good deal of time.

"'*Wasn't* it odd,' said Miss Lucy, one morning after breakfast, 'that Cecilia and the major should meet those Hicksons!'"

"'Who are the Hicksons?' I asked."

"'Oh! my dear girl, don't you remember, in Cecilia's last letter, her telling us about the lady she met in that shop when they were in town, buying a shawl the counterpart of her own? and it seems so odd they should turn up in Bath, and be such nice people! Don't you remember mamma said it must be the same family as that Colonel Hickson who was engaged to a girl with one eye, and she caught the small-pox and got so much marked, and he broke it off?'"

"'Small-pox and one eye would look very ugly,' Fatima languidly observed; and this subject drifted after the rest."

"One afternoon, I remember, it chanced that we were left alone with our hostess in the drawing-room. No one else happened to be in the way to talk to, and the good lady talked to us. We were clever girls for our age, I fancy, and we had been used to talk a good deal with our mother; at any rate we were attentive listeners, and I do not think our hostess required much more of us. I think she was glad of anybody who had not heard the whole affair from beginning to end, and so she put up her feet on the sofa, and started afresh with the complete history of her dear Cecilia from the cradle; and had gone on to the major, his military exploits abroad, his genteel connections at home, and the tendency to gout in the family which troubled him at times, and was a sad anxiety to her dear child, when visitors were announced.

"Our intelligent attention had gained favour for us; and we were introduced to these ladies as 'daughters of a very dear friend of mine, whom I have not seen for years,' on which one lady gave a sweet glance and a tight smile and murmured:

"'So pleasant to renew acquaintance in the children;' and the other ladies gave sweet glances, and tight smiles also, and echoed:

"'So pleasant!'"

"'Such sensible girls!' said our hostess, as if we were not there; 'like women of fifty. So like their dear mother! Such treasures to my little Lucy! You know she has lost her dear sister,' etc., etc.

"For then the ladies drew together, and our hostess having got a fresh audience, we retired to distant arm-chairs, a good deal bewildered."

"But to return to our first evening."

"Miss Lucy and we retired together, and no sooner had the drawing-room door closed behind us, than she wound her arms round our waists, and became as devoted as if we had been side by side the whole evening.

"'I'll tell you what I'll do, my dear girls,' she said when we reached our room; 'I'll come and sleep with you (there's lots of room for three), and then I can go on about Cecilia's affair, and if we don't finish to-night we can go on to-morrow morning before we get up. I always wake early, so I can call you. I'll come back when I'm ready for bed.'"

"And she vanished."

"We were in bed when she returned. Her hair had been undergoing some wonderful process, and was now stowed away under a large and elaborate night-cap.

"'Bedford was so slow,' said she; 'and then, you know, I got into bed, and let her tidy the room, and then when she was fairly gone, out I got, and here I am. We shall be as comfortable as possible; I'll be in the middle, and then I can have you on each side of me, my dear girls;' and in she sprang.

"'Did you notice this?' she asked, holding up her hand, and pointing out the edging on the sleeve of her night-dress; 'it's a new pattern; do you know it? Oh! my dears, the yards and yards of tatting that Cecilia had for her trousseau!'"

"Fatima and I were not rich in tatting edges, and rejoiced when the conversation took another turn."

"'About the proposal,' she rambled on; 'do you know I don't really know whereabouts Henry (that is the major, my brother-in-law,' she added, with one of the little attacks of dignity to which she was subject) 'proposed or what he said. I asked Cecy, but she wouldn't tell me. She was very cross, often; I'm very glad she's married. I think sisters ought to marry off as fast as they can; they never get on well in a house together, you know.'"

"I fairly gasped at this idea, and Fatima said bluntly:

Juliana Horatia Ewing

"'There are lots of us, and we get on.'"

"'Ah!' said Miss Lucy, in tones of wisdom; 'wait till you're a little older, and you'll see. Cecy was at school with two sisters who hated each other like poison, and they were obliged to dress alike, and the younger wore out her things much faster than the other one, but she was obliged to wear them till her sister's were done. She used to wish so her sister would marry, Cecy said, and the best fun is, now they're both in love with the same man. He's the curate of the church they go to.'"

"'Which of them is he in love with?' I asked."

"'Oh, neither that I know of,' said Miss Lucy, composedly. 'They don't know him, you know; but they sit close under the pulpit, and they have such struggles about which shall get into the corner of the pew that's nearest. Cecy and I weren't like that; but still I'm very glad she's married. Now wasn't it stupid of her not to tell me? I should never have told anybody, you know. And don't you wonder what gentlemen do say, and how they say it? He couldn't propose sitting, and I think standing would be very awkward. I suppose he knelt. Aunt Maria doesn't approve of gentlemen kneeling; she says it's idolatry. I think they must look very silly. Cecy wouldn't even tell me what he said. She said he spoke to mamma, and mamma said his conduct was highly honourable; but I think it was very stupid. Do you know, my dears, I have a cousin who was really married at Gretna Green? She married an officer. He was splendidly handsome; but people said things against him, and her parents objected. So they eloped, and then went to Wales, to such a lovely place! Wasn't it romantic? They quarrelled afterwards though; he lives abroad now. People ought to be careful. I shall be very careful myself; I mean to refuse the first few offers I get.'"

"And so Miss Lucy rambled on, perfectly unconscious of the melancholy and yet ludicrous way in which she degraded serious subjects, which she was not old enough to understand, or wise enough to reverence. We were too young then to see it fully, but her frivolity jarred upon us, though she amused us, and excited our curiosity. She was not worse than many other girls, with plenty of inquisitiveness and sharp sense, and not too much refinement and feeling; whose accomplishments are learnt from the 'first masters,' and whose principles are left to be picked up from gossip, servants, and second-rate books; digested by ignorant, inquisitive, and undisciplined minds.

"I won't try to recall any more of it, dear Ida. I remember it was a continuous stream of unedifying gossip, varied by small boastings about her own family. We've so many connections, was a favourite phrase of Miss Lucy's, and it seemed to mean a great deal. 'Do you like making trees?' she asked. I was getting sleepy, and without much thought replied, 'I love trees beyond anything, and I like growing oak trees in bottles.' Miss Lucy's, 'My dear girl, I mean family trees, genealogical trees,' was patronizing to scorn. 'Ours is in the spring drawer of the big oak cabinet in the drawing-room,' she added. 'We are descended from King Stephen.'"

"I believe I was the first to fall asleep that night. The last words I remember hearing were: 'We've so many connections.'"

"The next day's post brought news from Bath of more general interest to the household. The plans of Cecilia and the major were changed; they were coming to her mother's on the following Monday.

"'My dear girls, I *am* so glad!' said Miss Lucy; 'you'll see them. But you will have to move out of your room, I'm sorry to say.'"

"And for the next twelve hours Miss Lucy was more descriptive of her family glories in general, and of the glories of her sister and brother-in-law in particular, than ever."

"Sunday was a day of mixed experiences to us; some pleasant and some the reverse. Miss Lucy in her best clothes was almost intolerably patronizing, and a general stiffness seemed to pervade everything, the ladies' silk dresses included. After breakfast we dawdled about till it was time to dress for church, and as most of the ladies took about five minutes more than they had allowed for, it seemed likely that we should be late. At the last moment, Miss Lucy lost her Prayer Book, and it was not till another five minutes had gone in the search that she remembered having left it in church the Sunday before. This being settled we all stowed away in the carriages and drove off. It was only a short drive; but when we came in sight of the quaint little church there was no sound of bells, and it became evident that we were late. In the porch we shook out our dresses, the Irishman divided the burden of Prayer Books he had been gallantly bearing, our hostess turned back from the half-open door to say in a loud and encouraging whisper, 'It's only the Confession;' and we swept up the little church into a huge square pew.

"My dear Ida, I must tell you that we had been brought up to have a just horror of being late for service, this being a point on which my father was what is called 'very particular.' Fatima and I therefore felt greatly discomposed by our late and disturbing entrance, though we were in no way to blame. We had also been taught to kneel during the prayers, and it was with a most uncomfortable sensation of doubt and shame-facedness that we saw one lady after another sit down and bend her bonnet over her lap, and hesitated ourselves to follow our own customs in the face of such a majority. But the red-haired young lady seemed fated to help us out of our difficulties. She sank at once on her knees in a corner of the pew, her green silk falling round her; we knelt by her side, and the question was settled. The little Irishman cast a doubtful glance at her for a moment, and then sat down, bending his head deeply into his hat. We went through a similar process about responding, which did not seem to be the fashion with our hostess and her friends. The red-haired young lady held to her own customs, however, and we held with her. Our responses were the less conspicuous, as they were a good deal drowned by the voice of an old gentleman in the next pew. Diversity seemed to prevail in the manners of the congregation. This gentleman stood during prayers, balancing a huge Prayer Book on the corner of the pew, and responding in a loud voice, more devout than tuneful, keeping exact time with the parson also, as if he had a grudge against the clerk and felt it due to himself to keep in advance of him. I remember, Ida, that as we came in, he was just saying, 'those things which we ought *not* to have done,' and he said it in so terrible a voice, and took such a glance at us over his gold-rimmed spectacles, that I wished the massive pulpit-hangings would fall and bury my confusion. When the text of the sermon had been given out, our hostess rustled up, and drew the curtains well round our pew. Opposite to me, however, there was a gap through which I could see the old gentleman. He had settled himself facing the pulpit, and sat there gazing at the preacher with a rigid attention which seemed to say—'Sound doctrine, if you please; I have my eye on you.'"

"We returned as we came."

"'Is there afternoon service?' I asked Miss Lucy."

"'Oh, yes!' was the reply, 'the servants go in the afternoon.'"

"'Don't you?' I asked."

"'Oh, no!' said Miss Lucy, 'once is enough. You can go with the maids, if you want to, my dears,' she added, with one of the occasional touches of insolence in which she indulged.

"Afternoon arrived, and I held consultation with Fatima as to what we were to do."

"When once roused, Fatima was more resolute than I."

"'Of course we'll go,' said she; 'what's the use of having written out all our good rules and sticking at this? We always go twice at home. Let's look for Bedford.'"

"On which mission I set forth, but when I reached the top of the stairs I caught sight of the red-haired young lady, in her bonnet and shawl, standing at the open door, a Prayer Book in her hand. I dashed downstairs, and entered the hall just as the Irishman came into it by another door. In his hand was a Prayer Book also, and he picked up his hat, and went smiling towards her. But as he approached the young lady, she looked so much annoyed—not to say cross—that I hesitated to go forwards.

"'Are you going to church?' said the little Irishman, with a pleased look."

"'I don't know,' said the young lady, briefly, 'are you?'"

"'I was—' he began, and stopped short, looking puzzled and vexed."

"'Is no else going?' he asked, after a moment's pause."

"'No one else ever does go,' she said, impatiently, and moved into the hall."

"The Irishman coloured."

"'I am in the habit of going twice myself, though you may not think it,' he said, quietly; 'my poor mother always did. But I do not pretend to go to such good purpose as she did, or as you would, so if it is to lie between us—'and, without finishing his sentence, he threw his book (not too gently) on to the table, and, just lifting his hat as he passed her, dashed out into the garden.

"I did not at all understand this little scene, but, as soon as he was gone, I ran up to ask our friend if she were going to church, and would take us. She consented, and I went back in triumph to Fatima. As there was no time to lose, we dressed quickly enough; so that I was rather surprised, when we went down, to find the Irish gentleman, with his face restored to its usual good humour, standing by our friend, and holding her Prayer Book as well as his own. The young lady did not speak, but, cheerfully remarking that we had plenty of time before us, he took our books also, and we all set forth.

"I remember that walk so well, Ida! The hot, sweet summer afternoon—the dusty plants by the pathway—the clematis in the hedges (I put a bit into my Prayer Book, which was there for years)—the grasshoppers and flies that our dresses caught up from the long grass, and which reappeared as we sat during the sermon.

"The old gentleman was in his pew, but his glance was almost benevolent, as, in good time, we took our places. We (literally) *followed* his example with much heartiness in the responses; and, if he looked over into our pew during prayers (and from his position he could hardly avoid it), he must have seen that even the Irishman had rejected compromises, and that we all knelt together.

"There was one other feature of that service not to be forgotten. When the sermon was ended, and I had lost sight of the last grasshopper in my hasty rising, we found that there was to be a hymn. It was the old custom of this church so to conclude Evening Prayer. No one seemed to use a book—it was Bishop Ken's evening hymn, which everyone knew, and, I think, everyone sang. But the feature of it to us was when the Irishman began to sing From her startled glance, I think not even the red-haired young lady had known that he possessed so beautiful a voice. It had a clearness without effort, a tone, a truth, a pathos, such as I have not often heard. It sounded strangely above the nasal tones of the school-children, and the scraping of a solitary fiddle. Even our neighbour, who had lustily followed the rhythm of the tune, though without much varying from the note on which he responded, softened his own sounds and turned to look at the Irishman, who sang on without noticing it, till, in the last verse, he seemed disturbed to discover how many eyes were on him. Happily, self-consciousness had come too late. The hymn was ended.

"We knelt again for the Benediction, and then went back through the summer fields."

"The red-haired young lady talked very little. Once she said:

"'How is it we have never heard you sing?'"

"To which the Irishman replied:

"'I don't understand music, I sing by ear; and I hate 'company' performances. I will sing to you whenever you like.'"

"'Mary,' said Fatima, when we were in our room again, 'I believe those two will marry each other some day.'"

"'So do I,' I answered; 'but don't say anything about it to Lucy.'"

"'No, indeed!' said Fatima, warmly. So we kept this idea sacred from Miss Lucy's comments—why, I do not think either of us could have told in words.

'Pity, that pleasant impressions—pity, that most impressions— pass away so soon!

* * * * *

"The evening was not altogether so satisfactory as the afternoon had been. First, Miss Lucy took us to see her sister's wedding-presents, most of which were still here in her mother's keeping. They were splendid, and Miss Lucy was eloquent. From them we dawdled on into her room, where she displayed her own treasures, with a running commentary on matters of taste and fashion, which lasted till it was time to dress for the evening, when she made the usual inquiry, 'What shall you put on to-night, my dear girls?' and we blushed to own that there was nothing further of our limited toilettes to reveal.

"In the drawing-room, similar subjects of conversation awaited us. Our hostess and her friends did not seem to care much for reading, and, as they did not work on Sunday evening, they talked the more. The chatter ran chiefly upon the Bath fashions, and upon some ball which had been held somewhere, where somebody had been dressed after a manner that it appeared needful to protest against; whilst somebody else (a cousin of our hostess) was at all points so perfectly attired, that it seemed as if she should have afforded ample consolation for the other lady's defects.

"Upon the beauty of this cousin, her father's wealth, and her superabundant opportunities of matrimony, Miss Lucy enlarged to us, as we sat in a corner. Another of her peculiarities, by-the-by, was this. By her own account, all her relatives and friends were in some sense beautiful. The men were generally 'splendidly handsome;' the ladies, 'the loveliest creatures.' If not 'lovely,' they were 'stylish;' if nothing else, they were 'charming.' For those who were beyond the magic circle, this process was reversed. If pretty, they 'wanted style.' If the dress was beyond criticism, the nose, the complexion, the hand was at fault. I have met with this *trait* in other cliques, since then.

"My dear Ida, I wish to encourage no young lady of the hoydenish age of thirteen, in despising nice dressing and pretty looks and manners; or in neglecting to pick up any little hints which she may glean in such things from older friends. But there are people to whom these questions seem of such first importance, that to be with them when you are young and impressionable, is to feel every defect in your own personal appearance to be a crime, and to believe that there is neither worth, nor love, nor happiness (no life, in fact, worth living for) connected with much less than ten thousand a year, and 'connections.' Through some such ordeal we passed that evening, in seeing and hearing of all the expensive luxuries without which it seemed impossible to feed, dress, sleep, go out—in fact, exist; and all the equally expensive items of adornment, without which it appeared to be impossible to have (or at any rate retain) the respect and affection of your friends.

"Meanwhile, the evening slipped by, and our Sunday reading had not been accomplished. We had found little good habits less easy to maintain in a strange household than we had thought, and this one seemed likely to follow some others that had been allowed to slip. The red-haired young lady had been absent for about half an hour, and the Irishman had been prowling restlessly round the room, performing murderous-looking fidgets with the paper-knives, when she returned with a book in her hand, which she settled herself resolutely to read. The Irishman gave a comical glance at the serious-looking volume, and then, seating himself on a chair just behind her, found apparent peace in the effort to sharpen a flat ruler on his knees. The young lady read on. It was evident that her Sunday customs were not apt to be disturbed by circumstances.

"I began to feel uncomfortable. Fatima was crouched down near Lucy, listening to the history of a piece of lace. I waited some little time to catch her eye, and then beckoned her to me.

"'We haven't read,' I whispered."

"'Dare you go?' asked Fatima."

"'We ought,' I said."

"It required more daring than may appear. To such little people as ourselves it *was* rather an undertaking to cross the big drawing-room, stealing together over the soft carpet; to attack the large, smooth handle, open the heavy door, and leave the room in the face of the company. We did it, however, our confusion being much increased by the Irish gentleman, who jumped up to open the door for us. We were utterly unable to thank him, and, stumbling over each other in the passage, flew up to our own room like caged birds set free.

"Fatima drew out the pillows from the bed, and made herself easy on the floor. I found the book, and climbed into the window-seat. The sun was setting, the light would not last much longer; yet I turned over the pages slowly, to find the place, which was in the second part, thinking of the conversation downstairs. Fatima heaved a deep sigh among her cushions, and said: 'I wish we were rich.'"

"'I wish we were at home,' I answered."

"'When one's at home,' Fatima continued, in doleful tones, 'one doesn't feel it, because one sees nobody; but when one goes among other people, it *is* wretched not to have plenty of money and things. And it's no good saying it isn't,' she added, hurriedly, as if to close the subject.

"'It's getting dark,' I said."

"'I beg your pardon: go on,' sighed Fatima."

"I lifted up my voice, and read till I could see no longer. It was about the Valley of Humiliation through which Mr. Greatheart led Christiana and her children. The 'green valley, beautified with lilies,' in whose meadows the air was pleasant; where 'a man shall be free from the noise and from the hurryings of this life;' and where 'in former times men have met with angels.'"

"The last streaks of crimson were fading in the sky when I read the concluding lines of the shepherd-boy's song—

'Fulness to such a burden is,
That go on pilgrimage,
Here little, and hereafter bliss,
Is best from age to age.'

"'Here little, and hereafter bliss!'"

"It is not always easy to realize what one believes. One needs sometimes to get away from the world around, 'from the noise and from the hurryings of this life,' and to hear, read, see, or do something to remind one that there is a standard which is not of drawing-rooms; that petty troubles are the pilgrimage of the soul; that great and happy lives have been lived here by those who have had but little; and that satisfying bliss is not here, but hereafter.

"We went downstairs slowly, hand in hand."

"'I wonder what mother is doing?' said Fatima."

*　*　*　*　*

"The next day Miss Lucy very good-naturedly helped us to move our belongings into the smaller room we were now to occupy. It was in another part of the house, and we rather enjoyed the running to and fro, especially as Miss Lucy was gracious and communicative in the extreme.

"'This is the oldest part of the house,' she said, as we sat on the bed resting from our labours, for the day was sultry; 'and it breaks off here in an odd way. There are no rooms beyond this. There were some that matched the other side of the house, but they were pulled down.'"

"'Why?' we asked."

"'Well, there's a story about it, in the family,' said Miss Lucy, mysteriously. 'But it's a ghost story. I'll tell you, if you like. But some people are afraid of ghost stories. I'm not; but if you are, I won't tell it.'"

"Of course we declared we were not afraid. Sitting there together, on a sunny summer's afternoon, perhaps we were not.

"'It's years and years ago,' began Miss Lucy; 'you know the

place has belonged to another branch of our family for generations. Well, at last it came down to an old Mr. Bartlett, who had one daughter, who, of course, was to be the heiress. Well, she fell in love with a man whose name I forget, but he was of inferior family, and very queer character; and her father would not hear of it, and swore that if she married him he would disinherit her. She would have married the man in spite of this, though; but what he wanted was her money; so, when he found that the old man was quite resolute, and that there was no chance of his dying soon, he murdered him.'"

"We both exclaimed; for this sudden catastrophe fairly took away our breath. Miss Lucy's nerves were not sensitive, however, and she rattled on.

"'He smothered him in bed, and, as he was a very old man, and might easily have died in the night some other way, and as nothing could be proved, he got off. Well, he married the daughter, and got the property; but the very first evening after he took possession, as he was passing the door of the old man's room, he heard somebody breathing heavily inside, and when he looked in, there was the old father asleep in his bed.'"

"'Not really?' we said."

"'Of course not really,' said Miss Lucy, 'but so it was said. That's the ghost part of it. Well, do what he would, he never could get rid of the old man, who was always there asleep; so he pulled the rooms down, and at last he went abroad, and there both he and his wife died, and the property went to a cousin, who took the name of Bartlett.'"

"'How awful!' we murmured. But Miss Lucy laughed, and told us other family anecdotes, and the ghost story somewhat passed from our minds, especially as a little later we heard wheels, and, peeping from the landing window, beheld a post-chaise drive up.

"'It's Cecilia!' screamed Miss Lucy, and left us at once."

"I may as well say here, my dear Ida, that Cecilia and the major proved altogether different from our expectations. Cecilia, in travelling gear, taking off an old bonnet, begging for a cup of tea, and complaining in soft accents that butter was a halfpenny a pound dearer in Bath than at home, seemed to have no connection with that Cecilia into the trimmings of whose dresses bank-notes had recklessly dissolved. The major, an almost middle-aged man, of roughish exterior, in plain clothes, pulling his moustache over a letter that had arrived for him, dispelled our visions of manly beauty and military pomp even more effectually. Later on, we discovered that Cecilia was really pretty, soft, and gentle, a good deal lectured by her mother, and herself more critical of Miss Lucy's dress and appearance than that young lady had been of ours. The major proved kind and sensible. He was well-to-do and had 'expectations,' which facts shed round him a glory invisible to us. They seemed a happy couple; more like the rest of the world than we had been led to suppose.

"The new-comers completely absorbed our attention during the evening, and it was not till we were fairly entering the older part on the house on our way to bed, that the story of the old man's ghost recurred to my mind. It was a relief to meet Bedford at this point, to hear her cheerful good-night, and to see her turn into a room only two doors from ours. Once while we were undressing I said:

"'What a horrid story that was that Lucy told us.'"

"To which sensible Fatima made answer: 'Don't talk about it.'"

"We dismissed the subject by consent, got into bed, and I fell asleep. I do not quite know how far on it was into the night when I was roused by Fatima's voice repeating my name over and over again, in tones of subdued terror. I know nothing more irritatingly alarming, when one is young and nervous, than to be roused thus by a voice in which the terror is evident and the cause unknown.

"'What's the matter?' I asked."

"'Don't you hear?' gasped Fatima, in a whisper."

"If she had said at once that there was a robber under the bed, a burglar at the window, or a ghost in the wardrobe, I should have prepared for the worst, and it would have been less alarming than this unknown evil.

"'I hear nothing,' I said, pettishly. 'I wish you'd go to sleep, Fatima.'"

"'There!—now!' said Fatima."

"I held my breath, and in the silence heard distinctly the sound of some one snoring in an adjoining apartment."

"'It's only some one snoring,' I said."

"'Where?' asked Fatima, with all the tragedy in her voice unabated."

"'In the room behind us, of course,' I said, impatiently. 'Can't you hear?'"

"Fatima's voice might have been the voice of a shadow as she answered: '*There is no room there.*'"

"And then a cold chill crept over me also; for I remembered that the wall from behind which the snoring unmistakably proceeded was an outer wall. There had been the room of old Mr. Bartlett, which his son-in-law and murderer had pulled down. There he had been heard 'breathing heavily,' and had been seen asleep upon his bed, long after he was smothered in his own pillows, and his body shut up in the family vault. At least, so it was said, and at that particular moment we felt no comfort from the fact that Miss Lucy had said that 'of course it wasn't true.' I said something, to which Fatima made no reply, and I could feel her trembling, and hear a half-choked sob. I think fear for her overpowered my other alarm, and gave me a sort of strength.

"'Don't, dear,' I begged. 'Let's be brave. It must be something else. And there's nothing in the room. Let's go to Bedford. She's next door but one.'"

"Fatima could speak no more. By the moonlight through the blind, I jumped up, and half dragged, half helped her out of bed and across the room. Opening the door was the worst. To touch anything at such a moment is a trial. We groped down the passage; I felt the handle of the first door, and turned that of the second, and in we went. The window-blind of this room was drawn up, and the moonlight streamed over everything. A nest of white drapery covered one chair, a muslin dress lay like a sick ghost over a second, some little black satin shoes and web-like stockings were on the floor, a gold watch and one or two feminine ornaments lay on the table; and in the bed reposed—not Bedford, but our friend Kate, fast asleep, with one arm over the bed-clothes, and her long red hair in a pigtail streaming over the pillow. I climbed up and treated her as Fatima had treated me, calling her in low, frightened tones over and over again. She woke at last, and sat up.

"'You sprites! What is the matter?' she exclaimed."

"I stumbled through an account of our misfortunes, in the middle of which the young lady lay down, and before it was ended I believe she was asleep again. Poor Fatima, who saw nothing before us but to return to our room with all its terrors, here began to sob violently, which roused our friend once more, and she became full of pity.

"'You poor children!' she said, 'I'm so sleepy. I cannot get up and go after the ghost now; besides, one might meet somebody. But you may get into bed if you like; there's plenty of room, and nothing to frighten you.'"

"In we both crept, most willingly. She gave us the long tail of her hair, and said, 'If you want me, pull. But go to sleep, if you can!'—and, before she had well finished the sentence, her eyes closed once more. In such good company a snoring ghost seemed a thing hardly to be realized. We held the long plait between us, and, clinging to it as drowning men to a rope, we soon slept also.

"When we returned to our room next day, there was no snoring to be heard, and in the full sunshine of a summer morning our fright seemed so completely a thing of the past, that I persuaded myself to suggest that it might have been 'fancy' (Kate had already expressed her deliberate opinion to this effect), to which Fatima, whose convictions were of a more resolute type than mine, replied, 'What's the use of trying to believe what's not true? I heard it; and shall know that I heard it, if I live till I'm a hundred.'"

"In all correct ghost stories, when the hero comes down in the morning, valiant, but exhausted from the terrors of the night, to breakfast, his host invariably asks him how he slept. When we came down, we found Kate and the Irishman alone together in the breakfast-room. Now it certainly was in keeping with our adventure when he stepped forward, and, bowing profoundly, asked how we had passed the night; but, in spite of the gravity of his face, there was a twinkle in the big brown eyes which showed us that we were being made fun of; and I felt slightly indignant with our friend, who had faithfully promised not to betray us to Miss Lucy, and might, I thought, have saved us from the ridicule of the Irishman. The rest of the company began to assemble, however, and to our relief the subject was dropped. But though the Irishman kept our secret, we had every reason to suspect that he did not forget it; he looked terribly roguish through breakfast, and was only kept in order by Kate's severe glances.

"'Always breathe through the nose,' he suddenly began. 'It moderates the severity of the air, is less trying to the lungs, and prevents snoring.'"

"'Very true,' said the major, who was sensible, and liked instructive observations."

"'It may be laid down as an axiom,' continued the Irishman, gravely, 'that the man who snores is sure to disturb somebody; and also that the man who doesn't snore till he dies, is not likely to live to be a snoring ghost when he is dead.'"

"Kate looked daggers. The major laughed, and said, 'Let me give you some beef.' When he didn't understand a remark he always laughed, and generally turned the conversation to eatables, in which he was pretty safe; for food is common ground, and a slight laugh answers most remarks, unless at a serious meeting or a visit of condolence. A little later the Irishman asked: 'What's the origin of the expression to stir up with a long pole?' which turned the conversation to wild beasts. But he presently inquired: 'What's the meaning of

Juliana Horatia Ewing

putting a thing up the spout?'"

"'Pawning it,' said the major, promptly."

"'People pawn their family jewels sometimes,' said Pat. 'Did you ever hear of anybody pawning the family ghosts?' he asked, suddenly turning to me. I gave a distressed 'No,' and he continued in a whisper, 'You never saw a ghost up the spout?'"

"But, before I could answer, he caught Kate's eye, and, making a penitent face, became silent."

"We were in the drawing-room after breakfast, when the Irishman passed the window outside, whistling 'Kathleen Mavourneen.' We were sitting at Kate's feet, and she got up, and whispering, 'He's got something to show you, but he wouldn't let me tell,' went out into the garden, we following her.

"There we found the Irishman, with a long pole, which he was waving triumphantly in the air. He bowed as we approached.

"'This, young ladies,' he said, 'is the original long pole spoken of at the breakfast-table. With this I am about to stir up and bring forth for your inspection the living and identical ghost whose snoring disturbed your repose last night.'"

"The little Irishman's jokes reassured me. I guessed that he had found some clue to our mysterious noise; but with Fatima it was otherwise. She had been too deeply frightened to recover so easily. She clung tremblingly to me, as I was following him, and whispered 'I'd rather not.'"

"On her behalf I summoned courage to remonstrate."

"'If you please, sir,' I said, 'Fatima would rather not; and, if you please, don't tease us any more.'"

"The young lady added her entreaties, but they were not needed. The good-natured little gentleman no sooner saw Fatima's real distress than he lowered his pole, and sank upon his knees on the grass, with a face of genuine penitence.

"'I *am* so sorry I've been tormenting you so!' he exclaimed. 'I forgot you were really frightened, and you see I knew it wasn't a ghost.'"

"'I heard it,' murmured Fatima resolutely, with her eyes half shut."

"'So did I,' said the Irishman, gaily; 'I've heard it dozens of times. It's the owls.'"

"We both exclaimed."

"'Ah!' he said, comically, 'I see you don't believe me! That's what comes of telling so many small fibs. But it's true, I assure you. (And the brown eyes did look particularly truthful.) Barn-door owls do make a noise that is very like the snoring of an old man. And there are some young ones who live in the spout at the corner of the wall of your room. They're snoring and scrambling in and out of that spout all night.'"

"It was quite true, Ida, as we found, when Fatima was at last persuaded to visit the corner where the rooms had been pulled down, and where, decorated with ivy, the old spout formed a home for the snoring owls. By the aid of the long pole he brought out a young one to our view—a shy, soft, lovely, shadow-tinted creature, ghostly enough to behold, who felt like an impalpable mass of fluff, utterly refused to be kissed, and went savagely blinking back into his spout at the earliest possible opportunity. His snoring alarmed us no more."

"And the noise really was that?" said Ida.

"It really was, my dear."

"It's a splendid story," said Ida; "you see, I didn't go to sleep *this* time. And what became of everybody, please? Did the red-haired young lady marry the Irishman?"

"Very soon afterwards, my dear," said Mrs. Overtheway. "We kept up our friendship, too, in after life; and I have many times amused their children with the story of the Snoring Ghost."

REKA DOM

"What is home, and where, but with the loving?"

—FELICIA HEMANS

At last Ida was allowed to go out. She was well wrapped up, and escorted by Nurse in a short walk for the good of her health. It was not very amusing, but the air was fresh and the change pleasant, although the street did not prove quite that happy region it had looked from the nursery windows. Moreover, however strong one may fancy one has become indoors, the convalescent's first efforts out of doors are apt to be as feeble as those of a white moth that has just crept from the shelter of its cocoon, giddy with daylight, and trembling in the open air. By-and-by this feeling passed away, and one afternoon Ida was allowed to go by herself into the garden, "just for a run."

The expression was metaphorical, for she was far from being able to run; but she crept quietly up and down the walks, and gathered some polyanthuses, putting them to her face with that pleasure which the touch of fresh flowers gives to an invalid. Then she saw that the hedge was budding, and that the gap through which she had scrambled was filled up. Ida thought of the expedition and smiled. It had certainly made her very ill, but—it had led to Mrs. Overtheway.

The little old lady did not come that day, and in the evening
Ida was sent for by her uncle. She had not been downstairs in
the evenings since her illness. These interviews with the
reserved old gentleman were always formal, uncomfortable
affairs, from which Ida escaped with a sense of relief, and
that evening—being weak with illness and disappointed by
Mrs. Overtheway's absence—her nervousness almost
amounted to terror.

Nurse did her best in the way of encouragement. It was true
that Ida's uncle was not a merry gentleman, but there was
such a nice dessert! What could a well-behaved young lady
desire more than to wear her best frock, and eat almonds and
raisins in the dining-room, as if she were the lady of the
house?

"Though I am sorry for the child," Nurse confided to the
butler when she had left Ida with her uncle, "for his looks are
enough to frighten a grown person, let alone a little girl. And
do you go in presently, like a good soul, if you can find an
excuse, and let her see a cheerful face."

But before the kind-hearted old man-servant could find a
plausible pretext for intruding into the dining-room, and
giving an encouraging smile from behind his master's chair,
Ida was in the nursery once more.

She had honestly endeavoured to be good. She had made her
curtsey at the door without a falter—weak as she was. She
had taken her place at the head of the table with all dignity,
and had accepted the almonds and raisins with sufficiently
audible thanks. She had replied prettily enough to her uncle's
inquiries after her health; and, anxious to keep up the
conversation, had told him that the hedge was budding.

"*What's* the matter with the hedge?" he had asked rather sharply; and when Ida repeated her bit of spring news, he had not seemed to be interested. It was no part of the gardener's work.

Ida relapsed into silence, and so did her uncle. But this was not all. He had sharp eyes, and fierce bushy eyebrows, from under which he was apt to scrutinize Ida in a way that seemed to scatter all her presence of mind. This night of all nights she found his eyes upon her oftener than usual. Whenever she looked up he was watching her, and her discomfort increased accordingly. At last he broke the silence abruptly by saying:

"You were very sorry, child, were you not, when the news came of your father's death?"

The sudden introduction of this sacred subject made Ida's head reel.

"What?" she cried, and could get no further.

"Have you forgotten already?" the old gentleman said, almost reprovingly. "You did not know him, it is true; but you must remember hearing that your poor father had been drowned at sea?"

Ida's only reply was such a passionate outburst of weeping that her uncle rang the bell in helpless dismay, and was thankful when the old butler lifted the child tenderly in his arms and carried her back to Nurse. The old gentleman's feelings were more kindly than his looks, and he was really as much concerned as puzzled by the effect of his remarks. When the butler returned with the report that Ida was going quietly to bed, he sent her his "love" (the word seemed to struggle with some difficulty from behind his neck-cloth), and all the remaining almonds and raisins.

"I can't eat them," said Ida, smiling feebly, for her head was aching, "but it is very kind of him; and please tell Brown to tell him that I am very sorry, and please put the almonds and raisins into my box. I will make a dolls feast with them, if ever I make dolls' feasts again."

With which the weary little maid turned upon her pillow, and at last forgot her troubles in sleep.

The next morning Brown delivered a similar message from the old gentleman. He had gone away by an early train on business, but had left Ida his love.

"It's very kind of him," said Ida, again. But she went sadly on with some paper she was cutting into shapes. She was in low spirits this morning.

Comfort was at hand, however. In the course of the day there came a message from Mrs. Overtheway, asking Nurse to allow Ida to go to tea with her that evening. And Nurse consented.

Ida could hardly believe her senses when she found herself by the little old lady's own fireside. How dainty her room was! How full the bookshelves were! How many pictures hung upon the walls!

Above a little table, on which were innumerable pretty things, hung two pictures. One of these was a portrait of a man who, from his apparent age, might have been the old lady's son, but that he was not at all like her. He might have been good-looking, though, Ida thought, and he had a kind, intelligent face, full of energy and understanding, and that is better still. Close under his portrait hung a little sketch. It was of a road running by a river. Opposite to the river was a house and some trees. It was a pretty sketch, Ida thought, and the road looked interesting, as some roads do in pictures—making one wish to get into the frame and walk down them to see whither they lead. Below the sketch were some curious-looking characters written in ink, and of these Ida could make nothing.

Tea was soon ready. It was spread out on a little table by itself. The white cloth seemed to Ida the whitest she had ever seen, the silver and glass glittered, the china was covered with a rosebud pattern, and a reading-lamp threw a clear soft light over all. The tea, the cream, the brown bread and butter, the fresh eggs, and the honey—all were of the very best—even the waiting-maid was pretty, and had something of the old lady's smile.

When she had finished her duties by taking away the things, and putting the tea-table into a corner, the two friends drew up to the fire.

"You look better for tea, my child," said the little old lady. "Do you eat enough at home?"

"As much as I can," said Ida, "but I am more hungry when somebody else has tea with me. There very seldom was anybody till you came though. Only once or twice Lady Cheetham's housekeeper has been to tea. She is Nurse's father's first cousin, and 'quite the lady,' Nurse says. So she won't let her have tea in the kitchen, so both she and Nurse have tea in the nursery, and we have lots of tea-cakes and jam, and Nurse keeps saying, 'Help yourself, Miss Ida! Make yourself at home, Mrs. Savory!' And, you know, at other times, she's always telling me not to be all night over my tea. So I generally eat a good deal then, and I often laugh, for Nurse and Mrs. Savory are so funny together. But Mrs.

Juliana Horatia Ewing

Savory's very kind, and last time she came she brought me a pincushion, and the time before she gave me a Spa mug and two apples."

Mrs. Overtheway laughed, too, at Ida's rambling account, and the two were in high good-humour.

"What shall I do to amuse you?" asked the little old lady.

"You couldn't tell me another story?" said Ida, with an accent that meant, "I hope you can!"

"I would, gladly, my dear, but I don't know what to tell you about;" and she looked round the room as if there were stories in the furniture which perhaps there were. Ida's eyes followed her, and then she remembered the picture, and said:

"Oh! would you please tell me what the writing means under that pretty little sketch?"

The little old lady smiled rather sadly, and looked at the sketch in silence for a few moments. Then she said:

"It is Russian, my dear. Their letters are different from ours. The words are 'Reka Dom' and they mean 'River House.'"

Ida gazed at the drawing with increased interest.

"Oh, do you remember anything about it? If you would tell me about *that*!" she cried.

But Mrs. Overtheway was silent again. She was looking down, and twisting some of the rings upon her little hand, and Ida felt ashamed of having asked.

"I beg your pardon," she said, imploringly. "I was very rude, dear Mrs. Overtheway; tell me what you like, please."

"You are a good child," said the little old lady, "a very good child, my dear. I *do* remember so much about that house, that I fall into day-dreams when I look at it. It brings back the memories of a great deal of pleasure and a great deal of pain. But it is one advantage of being old, little Ida, that Time softens the painful remembrances, and leaves us the happy ones, which grow clearer every day."

"Is it about yourself?" Ida asked, timidly. She had not quite understood the little old lady's speech; indeed, she did not understand many things that Mrs. Overtheway said, but they were very satisfactory companions for all that.

"Yes, it is about myself. And since there is a dear child who cares about old Mrs. Overtheway, and her prosy stories, and all that befell her long ago," said the little old lady, smiling affectionately at Ida, "I will tell her the story—my story—the story of Reka Dom."

"Oh, how good of you!" cried Ida.

"There is not much merit in it," said the little old lady. "The story is as much for myself as you. I tell myself bits of it every evening after tea, more so now than I used to do. I look far back, and I endeavour to look far forward. I try to picture a greater happiness, and companionship more perfect than any I have known; and when I shall be able to realize them, I shall have found a better Home than Reka Dom."

Ida crept to the little old lady's feet, and softly stroked the slipper that rested on the fender. Then, while the March wind howled beyond the curtains, she made herself a cosy corner by the fire, and composed herself to hear the story.

"I remember," said Mrs. Overtheway. "I remember Reka Dom. It was our new home.

"Circumstances had made it necessary that we should change our residence, and the new home was to be in a certain quiet little town, not much bigger than some big villages—a town of pebble streets and small shops, silent, sunny, and rather dull—on the banks of a river.

"My health at this time was far from robust; but there is compensation even for being delicate in that spring-time of youth, when the want of physical strength is most irksome. If evening parties are forbidden, and long walks impossible, the fragile member of the family is, on the other hand, the first to be considered in the matter of small comforts, or when there is an opportunity for 'change of air.' I experienced this on the occasion when our new home was chosen. It had been announced to us that our father and mother were going away for one night, and that we were to be very good in the absence of those authorized keepers of the peace. We had not failed ourselves to enlarge this information by the discovery that they were going to the little town by the river, to choose the house that was to be our home; but it was not till the night before their departure that I was told that I was to go with them. I had been unusually drooping, and it was supposed that the expedition would revive me. My own joy was unbounded, and that of my brothers and sisters was hardly less. They were generously glad for my sake, and they were glad, also, that one of the nursery conclave should be on the spot when the great choice was made. We had a shrewd suspicion that in the selection of a house our elders would be mainly influenced by questions of healthy situation, due drainage, good water supply, moderate rent, and so forth; to the neglect of more important considerations, such as odd corners for hide-and-seek, deep window-seats, plenty of cupboards, and a garden adapted to the construction of bowers rather than to the cultivation of vegetables. I do not think my hopes of influencing the parental decision were great; but still we all felt that it was well that I should be there, and my importance swelled with every piece of advice I received from the rest of the party.

"'It must be a big house, but, of course, that adds to the expense,' said one of the older boys, who prided himself upon being more grown-up in his views than the rest, and considering the question from an elderly point of view. 'But if you don't take it out one way, you have it another,' he continued. A manly-sounding sentence, which impressed us all. 'Don't think about smartness, Mary,' he went on, with a grand air of renouncing vanities; 'fine entrance, you know, and front door. But a good back yard, if possible, and some empty outhouses for carpenters' shops; and if you could meet with a place with a few old boxes and barrels lying about, for rafts on the river and so forth, it would be a good thing.'"

"'I want a tidy box for a new baby-house, *dreadfully*,' added a sister."

"'I hope there'll be deep window-places,' sighed the luxurious Fatima, 'with print patchwork cushions, like those at the farm. And I hope some of them will face west, for the sunsets.'"

"'Above all'—and it was the final and most impressive charge I received—'whatever else is wanting, let us have two tall trees for a swing.'"

"Laden with responsibility, but otherwise light-hearted enough, I set out with my parents by the early coach, which was to put us down about mid-day in the little town by the river."

Juliana Horatia Ewing

"I liked travelling with my father. What a father he was! But, indeed, he was an object of such special devotion to me, and his character exercised so strong an influence over my young days, that I think, my dear Ida, that I must take the old woman's privilege of discursiveness, and tell you something about him.

"I remember that he was a somewhat mysterious personage in our young eyes. We knew little of his early life, and what we did know only enhanced the romantic mystery which we imagined to hang round it. We knew that he had seen many foreign lands, and in those days much travelling was rare. This accounted for the fact that, absent and somewhat unpractical as he was at home, he was invaluable on a journey, making arrangements, and managing officials with the precision of old habit. Where he had learnt his peculiar courtesy and helpfulness with those under his charge was less obvious. My mother said he had been accustomed to 'good society' in his youth, though we lived quietly enough now. We knew that, as a lad, he had been at sea, and sailors are supposed to be a handy and gentle-mannered race with the weak and dependent. Where else he had been, and what he had done, we did not exactly know; but I think we vaguely believed him to have been concerned in not a few battles by land and sea; to be deep in secrets of state, and to have lived on terms of intimacy with several kings and queens. His appearance was sufficiently striking to favour our dreams on his behalf. He had a tall, ungainly figure, made more ungainly by his odd, absent ways; but withal he was an unmistakable gentleman. I have heard it said of him that he was a man from whom no errors in taste could be feared, and with whom no liberties could ever be taken. He had thick hair of that yellow over which age seems to have no power, and a rugged face, wonderfully lighted up by eyes of rare germander blue. His hair sometimes seemed to me typical of his mind and tastes, which Time never robbed of their enthusiasm.

"With age and knowledge the foolish fancies I wove about my father melted away, but the peculiar affection I felt for him, over and above my natural love as a daughter, only increased as I grew up. Our tastes were harmonious, and we always understood each other; whereas Fatima was apt to be awed by his stateliness, puzzled by his jokes, and at times provoked by his eccentricities. Then I was never very robust in my youth; and the refined and considerate politeness which he made a point of displaying in his own family were peculiarly grateful to me. That good manners (like charity) should begin at home, was a pet principle with him, and one which he often insisted upon to us.

"'If you will take my advice, young people,' he would say, 'you will be careful never to let your sisters find other young gentlemen more ready and courteous, nor your brothers find other young ladies more gentle and obliging than those at home.'"

"My father certainly practised what he preached, and it would not have been easy to find a more kind and helpful travelling companion than the one with whom my mother and I set forth that early morning in search of our new abode."

"I was just becoming too much tired to care to look any longer out of the window, when the coach rumbled over the pebbly street into the courtyard of the 'Saracen's Head.'"

"I had never stayed at an inn before. What a palace of delights it seemed to me! It is true that the meals were neither better nor better cooked than those at home, and that the little room devoted to my use was far from being as dainty as that which Fatima and I habitually shared; but the

Juliana Horatia Ewing

keen zest of novelty pervaded everything, and the faded chintz and wavy looking-glass of No. 25 are pleasant memories still. Moreover, it had one real advantage over my own bedroom. High up, at the back of the house, it looked out and down upon the river. How the water glittered and sparkled! The sun was reflected from its ripples as if countless hosts of tiny naiads each held a mirror to catch his rays. My home had been inland, and at some distance from a river, and the sight of water was new and charming to me. I could see people strolling along the banks; and then a boat carrying sails of a rich warm brown came into view and passed slowly under my eye, with a stately grace and a fair wind. I was watching her with keen interest, when I was summoned to dinner.

"Here, again, novelty exercised its charm. At home I think I may say that the nursery party without exception regarded dinner in the light of a troublesome necessity of existence. We were apt to grudge the length and formalities of the meal; to want to go out, or not to want to come in; or possibly the dining-room had been in use as a kite manufactory, or a juvenile artist's studio, or a doll's dressmaker's establishment, and we objected to make way for the roast meat and pudding. But on this occasion I took an interest in the dignities of the dinner-table, and examined the plates and dishes, and admired the old-fashioned forks and spoons, and puzzled over the entwined initials on their handles.

"After dinner we went out into the town, and looked through several houses which were to let. My high hopes and eager interest in the matter were soon quenched by fatigue; but faithful to my promise, I examined each house in turn. None of them proved satisfactory to my parents, and they were even less so to me. They were all new, all commonplace, and all equally destitute of swing-trees, interesting corners, deep window-seats, or superannuated boxes. Heat, fatigue, and disappointment at last so overpowered me that my pale face attracted notice, and my father brought me back to the inn. He carried me upstairs to the sofa, and, pointing out a bookshelf for my amusement, and telling me to order tea if I wished for it, went back to my mother.

"It was a shabby little collection of volumes, that parlour library in the 'Saracen's Head.' There was an old family Bible, a torn copy of 'Culpepper's 'Herbal,' the Homilies in inexpressibly greasy black calf, a book of songs, a volume called 'Evelina,' which seemed chiefly remarkable for dashes and notes of admiration, and—the book I chose.

"The book I chose would look very dull in your eyes, I dare say, my dear Ida; you who live in an age of bright, smart story-books, with clear type, coloured pictures, and gorgeous outsides. You don't know what small, mean, inartistic 'cuts' enlivened your grandmother's nursery library, that is, when the books were illustrated at all. You have no idea how very little amusement was blended with the instruction, and how much instruction with the amusement in our playbooks then, and how few there were of them, and how precious those few were! You can hardly imagine what a treasure I seemed to have found in a volume which contained several engravings the size of the page, besides many small wood-cuts scattered through the letter-press. I lost sight alike of fatigue and disappointment, as I pored over the pictures, and read bits here and there.

"And such charming pictures there were! With quaint anglers in steeple-crowned hats, setting forth to fish, or breakfasting under a tree (untrammelled by the formalities of a nursery meal), or bringing their spoils to a wayside inn with a painted fish upon the sign-board, and a hostess in a high hat and a stiff-bustled dress at the door. Then there were small wood-cuts which one might have framed for a doll's house;

portraits of fish of all kinds, not easily distinguishable by the unpractised eye; and nicer wood-cuts still of country scenes, and country towns, and almost all of these with a river in them. By the time that my father and mother returned, I had come to the conclusion that the bank of a river was, of all situations, the most desirable for one's home, and had built endless bowers in the air like that in which the anglers are seated in the picture entitled 'The Farewell;' and had imagined myself in a tall hat and a stiff-bustled dress cooking fish for my favourite brothers after the recipes in Walton and Cotton's 'Complete Angler.'"

"They came back with disappointment on their faces. They had not got a house, but my mother had got a headache, and we sat down to tea a dispirited party.

"It is sometimes fortunate as well as remarkable, how soon everybody knows everything about everybody else, especially in a small town. As the tea-things went downstairs, our landlord came up to help us in our difficulty. Had the gentleman succeeded in obtaining a house? If none of the new lot suited him, the landlord believed that one or more of older date were to let near the river. It was not the fashionable quarter, but there had been well-to-do people and some good substantial residences there.

"Our hopes rose again, and the idea of an old and substantial residence in an unfashionable quarter was so much more favourable to nursery interests than the smart gimcrack houses at which we had been looking, that I should have been anxious to explore that part of the town to which he directed us, even if it had not possessed a charm that was now pre-eminent in my eyes. It was near the river.

"My mother was too much tired to attempt further investigations, but I had completely recovered from my fatigues, and was allowed to go with my father on the new search. He and I were very good company, despite the difference in age between us. We were never in each other's way, and whether we chatted or did not speak, we were happy together, and enjoyed ourselves in our respective fashions.

"It was a lovely evening. Hand in hand we turned out of the 'Saracen's Head' into the shingly street, took the turning which led to the unfashionable quarter, and strolled on and on, in what Scott calls 'social silence.' I was very happy. It was not only a lovely evening—it was one of these when the sunlight seems no longer mere sunlight, but has a kind of magical glow, as if a fairy spell had been cast over everything; when all houses look interesting—all country lanes inviting—when each hedge, or ditch, or field seems a place made to play in at some wonderful game that should go on for years.

"As we wandered on, we passed a line of small bright-looking houses, which strongly caught my fancy. Each had its gay little garden, its shrubbery of lilac, holly, or laurustinus, and its creeper-covered porch. They looked so compact and cosy, so easy to keep tidy, so snug and sunny, that one fancied the people who lived in them must be happy, and wondered who they were.

"'Oh, father!' I exclaimed, 'what delightful houses!'"

"'They are very pretty, my dear,' he answered; 'but they are much too small for us; besides which, they are all occupied.'"

"I sighed, and we were passing on, when I held him back with another exclamation."

"'Oh! *look* at the carnations!' For in one of the gardens large

Juliana Horatia Ewing

clumps of splendid scarlet cloves caught my eye."

"My father humoured me, and we drew near to the laurustinus hedge, and looked over into the gay little garden. As we looked, we became conscious of what appeared like a heap or bundle of clothing near one of the beds, which, on lifting itself up, proved to be a tall slender lady of middle age, who, with her dress tucked neatly round her, a big print hood on her head, and a trowel in her hand, was busily administering such tender little attentions as mothers will lavish on their children, and garden lovers on their flowers. She was not alone in the garden, as we soon perceived. A shorter and stouter and younger lady sat knitting by the side of a gentleman in a garden-chair, who from some defect in his sight, wore a large green shade, which hid the greater part of his face. The shade was made of covered pasteboard, and was large and round, and so very like a lamp shade, that I hardly ever look at one of those modern round globe lamps, my dear, if it has a green shade, without being reminded of old Mr. Brooke.

"'Was that his name?' Ida asked."

"'Yes, my dear; but that we did not know till afterwards. When the good lady lifted herself up, she saw us, and seemed startled. My father raised his hat, and apologized politely. 'My little girl was so much taken with your carnations, madam,' he said, 'that we made bold to come near enough to look at them, not knowing that any one was in the garden.'"

"She seemed rather flustered, but pushed back her hood, and made a stiff little curtsey in answer to my father's bow, and murmured something about our being welcome.

"'Would you care to have some, my dear?' she added, looking at me. I gave a delighted assent, and she had gathered two lovely carnations, when we heard a quavering voice from under the green shade inquire—

"'What is it?'"

"Our friend was at the old gentleman's side in a moment, speaking very distinctly into his ear, as if he were deaf, whereby we heard her answer,

"'It's a gentleman and his little daughter, James, admiring our carnations, and I am gathering a few for the young lady, dear James.'"

"'Quite right, quite right,' he croaked. 'Anything that we have. Anything that we have.'"

"It was a great satisfaction to me afterwards to remember that my father had thanked these good people 'properly,' as I considered. As for myself, I had only been able to blush and stammer out something that was far from expressing my delight with the lovely nosegay I received. Then the slender lady went back to her gardening. Her sister took up the knitting which she had laid down, the old gentleman nodded his lamp-shade in the direction where he supposed us to be and said, 'Good evening, sir, Good evening, miss;' and we went our way.

"The road wound on and on, and down and down, until we found ourselves on the edge of the river. A log lay conveniently on the bank, and there we seated ourselves. The tide was out, and the river bed was a bed of mud except for a narrow stream of water that ran down the middle. But, ah! how the mud glistened in the evening sunshine which was reflected on it in prismatic colours. Little figures were dotted here and there over its surface, and seawards the masts of some vessels loomed large through the shining haze.

"'How beautiful everything looks this evening!' I exclaimed."

"'I see them walking in an air of glory,' murmured my father, dreamily."

"He was quoting from a favourite old poem, which begins—

'They are all gone into a world of light,
And I alone sit lingering here.'"

"This 'air of glory,' indeed, was over everything. The mud and the tide pools, the dark human figures, the black and white seagulls that sat like onyx pebbles on the river bed, the stream that spread seawards like a silver scroll, the swans that came sailing, sailing down the stream with just such a slow and stately pace as white-winged ships might have come down the river with the tide, to pass (as the swans did pass) into that 'world of light,' that shining seaward haze, where your eye could not follow them unless shaded by your hand.

"I do not quite know how long we sat gazing before us in silent enjoyment. Neither do I know what my father's thoughts were, as he sat with his hands clasped on his knees and his blue eyes on the river. For my own part, I fancied myself established in one of the little houses as 'hostess,' with a sign-board having a fish painted upon it hanging outside the door, and a bower of woodbine, sweet-briar, jessamine, and myrtle commanding a view of the river. The day dream was broken by my father's voice.

"'Mary, my dear, we must go about our business, or what will your mother say to us? We must see after these houses. We can't live on the river's bank.'"

"'I wish we could,' I sighed; and though he had risen and

turned away, I lingered still. At this moment my father exclaimed—

"'Bless my soul!' and I jumped up and turned round."

"He was staring at a wall with a gateway in it, enclosing a house and garden on the other side of the road. On the two gateposts were printed in black Roman letters two words that I could not understand—*Reka Dom*.

"'What does it mean?' I asked."

"'Reka Dom?' said my father thoughtfully (and he pronounced it *Rayka Dome*). 'It is Russian. It means River House. Very curious! I suppose the people who live here are Russians. It's a nice situation—a lovely view—*lovely*!' and he had turned round to the river, but I caught his arm.

"'Father, dear, no one lives here. Look!' and I pointed to a board beyond the gateway, which stated in plain English that the house was to let."

* * * * *

"By the time that we returned to my mother, Reka Dom was to all intents and purposes our home."

"It is true that the house was old, rambling, and out of repair, and that what we heard of the landlord was not encouraging. He was rich, we were told, but miserly; and 'a very queer old gentleman,' whose oddness almost amounted to insanity. He had 'made himself so unpleasant' to various people who had thought of taking the house, that they drew back, and Reka Dom had been untenanted for some time. The old woman who took care of it, and from whom we got this information, prophesied further that he would 'do nothing to the old place.

He'd let it fall about his ears first.'"

"It is also true that standing in the garden (which in its rambling, disorderly way was charming, and commanded a lovely view), my father rubbed his head ruefully, and said:

"'You know, Mary, your mother's chief objection to our latest home was that the grounds were so much too large for our means of keeping them in order; and this garden is the larger of the two, I fear.'"

"And he did not seem to derive proportionate comfort from my reply."

"'But, father dear, you know you needn't keep it in order, and then we can have it to play in.'"

"And yet we took Reka Dom."

"The fact is that my father and I took a fancy to the place. On my side this is easily to be accounted for. If all the other houses at which we had looked had proved the direct reverse of what I (on behalf of myself and my brothers and sisters) was in search of, Reka Dom in a remarkable degree answered our requirements. To explore the garden was like a tour in fairy land. It was oddly laid out. Three grass-plots or lawns, one behind another, were divided by hedges of honeysuckle and sweet-briar. The grass was long, the flower-borders were borders of desolation, where crimson paeonies and some other hardy perennials made the best of it, but the odour of the honeysuckle was luxuriously sweet in the evening air. And what a place for bowers! The second lawn had greater things in store for me. There, between two tall elm trees hung a swing. With a cry of delight I seated myself, seized the ropes, and gave a vigorous push. But the impetus was strong, and the ropes were rotten, and I and the swing came to the ground together. This did not deter me, however, from exploring the third lawn, where I made a discovery to which that of the swing was as nothing.

"It was not merely that a small path through the shrubbery led me into a little enclosed piece of ground devoted to those many-shaped, box-edged little flower-beds characteristic of 'children's gardens,'—it was not alone that the beds were shaped like letters, and that there was indisputably an M among them—but they were six in number. Just one apiece for myself and my brothers and sisters! And though families of six children are not so very uncommon as to make it improbable that my father's predecessor should have had the same number of young ones as himself, the coincidence appeared to my mind almost supernatural. It really seemed as if some kind old fairy had conjured up the whole place for our benefit. And—bless the good godmother!—to crown all, there were two old tea-chests and a bottomless barrel in the yard.

"Doubtless many causes influenced my father in *his* leaning towards Reka Dom, and he did not confide them to me. But I do truly believe that first and foremost of the attractions was its name. To a real hearty lover of languages there is a charm in the sight of a strange character, new words, a yet unknown tongue, which cannot be explained to those who do not share the taste. And perhaps next to the mystic attraction of words whose meaning is yet hidden, is to discover traces of a foreign language in some unexpected and unlikely place. Russian is not extensively cultivated; my father's knowledge of it was but slight, and this quiet little water-side town an unlikely place for an inscription in that language. It was curious, and then interesting, and then the quaint simple title of the house took his fancy. Besides this, though he could not but allow that there was reason in my mother's views on the subject of large grounds in combination with one man-of-all-work, he liked plenty of space and shrubbery where he could

Juliana Horatia Ewing

wander about—his hands behind his back—without being disturbed; and for his own part he had undoubtedly felt more pleasure in the possession of large grounds than annoyance at seeing them neglected. So the garden tempted him. Finally, there was a room opening upon a laurel walk, which had at one time been a library. The shelves—old, common, dirty and broken—were still there, and on the most secure of them the housekeeper kept her cheese and candles, and an old shawl and bonnet.

"'The place is made for us!' I exclaimed on my return from discovering the old barrel and tea-chests. My father was standing in the library looking out upon the garden, and he did not say No.

"From the old woman we learnt something of the former tenants. She was a good-natured old soul, with an aggrieved tone of voice, due probably to the depressing effects of keeping an empty house for a cantankerous landlord. The former tenant's name was Smith, she said (unmistakably English this!). But his lady was a *Roosian*, she believed. They had lived in *Roosia*, and some of the children, having been born there, were little *Roosians*, and had *Roosian* names. She could not speak herself, having no knowledge of the country, but she had heard that the *Roosians* were heathens, though Mr. Smith and his family went regularly to church. They had lived by a river, she believed, and their old home was called by the same outlandish name they had given to this. She had heard that it meant a house by the water-side, but could not say, knowing no language but her own, and having (she was thankful to say) found it sufficient for all purposes. She knew that before Mr. Smith's time the house was called Montague Mount, and there was some sense in that name. Though what the sense was, she did not offer to explain.

"'Please, please take it!' I whispered in a pause of the conversation! 'there are six little gardens, and—'"

"My father broke in with mock horror on his face: 'Don't speak of six gardens!' he exclaimed. 'The one will condemn the place, I fear, but we must go home and consult your mother.'"

"I suppose we did consult her."

"I know we described all the charms of the house and garden, and passed rather a poor examination as to their condition, and what might be expected from the landlord. That my father endeavoured to conceal his personal bias, and that I made no secret of mine. At last my mother interrupted some elaborately practical details by saying in her gentle voice—

"'I think choosing a home is something like choosing a companion for life. It is chiefly important to like it. There must be faults everywhere. Do you take to the place, my dear?'"

"'I like it certainly,' said my father. 'But the question is not what I like, but what you like.'"

"Then I knew it was settled, and breathed freely. For though my father always consulted my mother's wishes, she generally contrived to choose what she knew he would prefer. And she chose Reka Dom.

*　*　*　*　*

"Henceforward good luck seemed to follow our new home."

"First, as to the landlord. The old woman had certainly not

exaggerated his oddity. But one of his peculiarities was a most fortunate one for us. He was a bibliomaniac—a lover and collector of valuable and curious books. When my father called on him to arrange about the house, he found him sitting almost in rags, apparently dining upon some cheese-parings, and surrounded by a library, the value of which would have fed and clothed him with comfort for an almost indefinite period. Upon the chair behind him sat a large black cat with yellow eyes.

"When my father was ushered in, he gazed for a moment in silent astonishment at the unexpected sight. Books in shelf after shelf up to the ceiling, and piled in heaps upon the floor. As he stood speechless, the little old man put down the plate, gathered his ragged dressing-gown about him, and, followed by the cat, scrambled across the floor and touched his arm.

"'You look at books as if you loved them?' he said."

"My father sighed as if a spell had been broken."

"'I am nearly half a century old,' he said, 'and I do not remember the day when I did not love them.'"

"He confessed afterwards to my mother that not less than two hours elapsed before Reka Dom was so much as spoken of. Then his new acquaintance was as anxious to secure him for a tenant as he had been to take the house.

"'Put down on paper what you think wants doing, and it shall be done,' was the old gentleman's liberal order on the subject of repairs. 'Lord! Lord!' he went on, 'it's one thing to have you, and another thing to put the house right for men who don't know an Elzevir from an annual in red silk. One fellow came here who would have given me five pounds more than

I wanted for the place; but he put his vile hat upon my books. Lord! Lord!'

"The old man's strongest effort in my father's favour, however, was the proposal of a glass of wine. He seemed to have screwed himself up to the offer, and to be proportionately relieved when it was declined.

"'You're quite right,' he said, frankly; 'my wine is not so good as my books. Come and see them, whenever you like.'"

"'The bookshelves shall be repaired, sir,' was his final promise in answer to a hint from my father, who (it being successful, and he being a very straight-forward man) was ever afterwards ashamed of this piece of diplomacy. 'And the fire-place must be seen to. Lord! Lord! A man can live anywhere, but valuable books must be taken care of. Would you believe it? I have a fire in this room three times a week in bad weather. And fuel is terribly dear, terribly dear. And that slut in the kitchen burns as much as if she had the care of the Vatican Library. She said she couldn't roast the meat without. "Then give me cold meat!" I said; but she roasts and boils all the same. So last week I forbade the butcher the house, and we've lived on cheese ever since, and *that's* eightpence a pound. Food is terribly dear here, sir; everything is dear. It's enough to ruin a man. And you've got a family. Lord! Lord! How a man can keep a family and books together, I can't imagine. However, I suppose children live chiefly on porridge.'"

"Which supposition served for long as a household joke against my brothers, whose appetite for roast meat was not less than that of other healthy boys of the period."

"It was a happy moment when my father came back from this interview, and Reka Dom was fairly ours. But a more

Juliana Horatia Ewing

delightful one was that in which I told the successful result of my embassy to the nursery conclave. I certainly had not the remotest claim to credit in the matter, but I received an ovation proportionate to the good news I brought. I told my story skilfully, and made the six gardens the crowning point; at which climax my brother and sisters raised a shout that so far exceeded the average of even nursery noises, that my mother hurried to the spot, where our little sister Phil flung herself into her arms, and almost sobbing with excitement, cried—

"'Oh, Mother dear! we're *hooraying* for Reka Dom!'"

*   *   *   *   *

"It was sagely prophesied by our nurse and others that we should soon be tired of our new fancy, and find 'plenty to complain of' in Reka Dom as elsewhere. (It is nursery wisdom to chasten juvenile enthusiasm by such depressing truths.) And undoubtedly both people and places are apt to disappoint one's expectations on intimate acquaintance; but there are people and places who keep love always, and such an one was Reka Dom.

"I hardly know what to tell you of it, Ida. The happy years we spent there were marked by no wonderful occurrences, and were not enlivened by any particular gaiety. Beyond our own home our principal treat was to take tea in the snug little house where we made our first acquaintances. Those good ladies proved kind friends to us. Their buns were not to be surpassed, and they had pale albums, and faded treasures of the preceding generation, which it was our delight to overhaul. The two sisters lived with their invalid brother, and that was the household. Their names were Martha and Mary, and they cherished a touching bit of sentiment in reference to the similarity between their circumstances and those of the

Family of Bethany.

"'I think it reminds us of what we ought to be, my dear,' Miss Mary said to me one day. 'Only it is I who should have been called Martha, for Martha is far more spiritually minded.' Humility was the most prominent virtue in the character of these good ladies, and they carried it almost to excess.

"I remember, as a child, thinking that even the holy sisters of Bethany could hardly have been more good than the Misses Brooke, but I was quite unable to connect any sentiment with the invalid brother. He spoke little and did less, and yet his sisters continually quoted his sayings and criticisms, and spoke of his fine taste and judgment; but of all that he was supposed to say, only a few croaking common-places ever met our ears.

"'Dear James was so much pleased with that little translation you showed me,' or 'Dear James hopes that his young friends keep up their practising. He considers music such a resource,' etc., etc.

"I believe they did hold conversations with him in which he probably assented to their propositions, and they persuaded themselves that he was very good company. And, indeed, he may have been all that they believed; I can only say that to me dear James's remarks never exceeded, 'Good-day, Miss. How are your excellent parents?' or some similar civility. I really was afraid of him. There is something appalling in a hoarse voice coming from under a green shade, and connected with eyes you cannot meet, and features that are always hidden. Beyond that shade we never saw to the day of his death.

"This occurred about four years after we first knew them. I well remember the visit of condolence on which I accompanied my mother, the bitter grief of the sisters, and the slow dropping of Miss Mary's tears on to her black dress. Wonderful indeed is love! The most talented and charming companion in the world could not have filled to them the place of the helpless, uninteresting invalid who had passed away.

"The Misses Brooke caused a commotion in the gossiping world of our little town by going to the funeral. It was not the custom for ladies to go to funerals, and, as a general rule, the timid sisters would not have ventured to act against public opinion; but on this occasion they were resolute. To hear the voice of authority meet them with the very words wherewith Divine lips had comforted those other sisters, would comfort them, as nothing else could. I remember how from a window we watched the funeral with childish awe and curiosity—the thrill with which we heard a maid announce 'the coffin,' and caught sight of the flapping pall, and tried to realize that old Mr. Brooke was underneath. Then close behind it came the two figures we knew so well, veiled, black, and bent, and clinging together in the agony of that struggle between faith and loss which every loving soul is some time called on to endure. As we leant out of the open window, crying bitterly in sympathy with them, and with the gloomy excitement of the occasion, they raised themselves a little and walked more steadily. The Rector's clear voice was cutting the air with the pathos of an unusual sympathy.

'I am the Resurrection and the Life—saith the Lord.'"

"I understood then, and have never wondered since, how it was that the Misses Brooke braved the gossip of the neighbourhood, and followed their brother's body to the grave.

"These good people were, as I have said, our chief friends;

but Reka Dom itself afforded us ample amusement. The six children who had lived there before us were a source of unfailing interest. The old woman of the house remained about the place for a short time in the capacity of charwoman, and she suffered many inquiries on our part as to the names, ages, and peculiarities of our predecessors. As she had 'charred' for them, she was able to satisfy our curiosity to a considerable extent, and then great was the pleasure of retailing to our mother, as she sat knitting in the twilight, the anecdotes we had collected of 'the little Russians.'"

"'The Little Russians' certainly did much to cement our attachment to Reka Dom. Their history was the history of our home. It was the romance of the walks we played in, the swing we sat in, the gardens we tended every day. To play at being the little Russians superseded all other games. To 'pretend' that the little Russians were with us, and to give dolls' entertainments in their honour, supplanted all former fancies. Their gardens, by-the-by, were not allotted to their successors without some difficulty, and the final decision involved a disappointment to me. It seemed as if there could not be two opinions as to the propriety of my having the letter M. But on further consideration it appeared that as the remaining letters did not fit the names of my brothers and sisters, some other way of distributing them must be found. My mother at last decided that the letters of the six beds were to be written on six separate bits of paper, and put in a bag, and that one was to be drawn by each in turn. I still hoped that I might draw the letter M, but it was not to be. That large and sunny bed fell to my youngest brother, and I drew the letter I. Now not only was the bed little more than a fourth of the size of that which I had looked on as my own, but being very much in the shade, it was not favourable to flowers. Then the four divisions of the letter M afforded some scope for those effective arrangements which haunt one's spring dreams for the coming summer; but what could

Juliana Horatia Ewing

be done with a narrow strip with two narrower ends where the box-edging almost met, and where nothing would blossom but lilies of the valley?

("Capricious things those lilies are! So obdurate under coaxing when transplanted to some place they do not like, so immovably flourishing in a home that suits them!)

"What I did was to make the best of my fate. After trying to reduce the lilies of the valley to one neat group, and to cultivate gayer flowers in the rest of the bed, and after signally failing in both attempts, I begged a bit of spare ground in the big garden for my roses and carnations, and gave up my share of the Russian plat to the luxuriant lilies.

"It had belonged to the eldest boy. One of those born in Russia, and with the outlandish names of which the charwoman spoke. His name was Ivan. Many a time did I wish it had been William or Matthew, and once, I remember, I dreamt a tantalizing dream of discovering that it was Oliver, and of digging up the middle of the O, and effecting a round bed of unrivalled brilliancy, with a white rose for the centre-piece and crown. Once in the year, however, I had my revenge. In spring my lilies of the valley were the finest to be seen. We had a custom that all through the flower season a bouquet was laid by my mother's plate before she came down to breakfast, and very proud we were when they came from our own gardens. There were no horticultural wonders in these nosegays, but in my short season of triumph, the size and fragrance of my flowers never failed to excite admiration; and many grown-up people besides my mother were grateful for bouquets from my narrow bed. Credit in the matter I deserved none, for Ivan's lilies took care of themselves.

"Having learnt the names of the little Russians, we had no difficulty in discovering to which of them the respective letter beds had belonged; and one of our amusements was that each should endeavour to carry out what (so far as we could learn) had been the habits and customs of the little Russian to whose garden he had succeeded. Then we had a whole class of partisan games which gave us wonderful entertainment. Sometimes we pretended to be Scottish chieftains, or feudal barons of England, or chiefs of savage tribes. Our gardens were always the lands we had inherited or conquered, and we called ourselves by the names of the little Russians. When we were Highland chiefs, I remember, we put Mac indiscriminately before all the names; in some cases with a comical, and in others with a very satisfactory effect. As chief of the MacIvans I felt justly proud of my title, but a brother who represented the MacElizabeths was less fortunate. In the sham battles our pet animals (we each had one) did duty for retainers, much to their bewilderment. The dogs, indeed, would caper about, and bark round the opposing parties in a way that was at least inspiriting; but my Sandy Tom brandished his tail and took flying leaps upon no principle whatever; and as to Fatima's tortoise, it never budged from the beginning of the conflict to the end. Once, indeed, by strewing dandelion heads in the direction of the enemy's ground she induced him to advance, and at the cry of 'Forward, MacPeters!' he put forth a lazy leg, and with elephantine dignity led the attack, on the way to his favourite food. But (in spite of the fable) his slow pace was against him, and in the ensuing *melee* he was left far behind.

"I could not learn much about Ivan, but of what I did discover some things were easy enough for me to follow. He was fond of boating, a taste I was not allowed to cultivate; but also he was fond of books, the old woman said, and fond of sitting in the swing and reading, and I heartily approved his choice in this respect.

"In helping to unpack my father's library, I had discovered a copy of Walton and Cotton's 'Angler,' similar in every respect, but its good condition, to the one that had charmed me at the inn. Sometimes the precious volume was lent to me, and with it in my lap, and my arms round the ropes of the swing, I passed many a happy hour. What fancies I wove after studying those quaint, suggestive old prints! As sweet as that 'contexture of woodbines, sweet-briar, and myrtle' in which the anglers sat and sipped orange punch at Tottenham. The characters of *Piscater*, *Venater*, and *Auceps*, and the style of their conversations by the wayside, I found by no means unlike those of the Pilgrim's Progress. The life-like descriptions of nature (none the less attractive at my age from being quaintly mixed with fable and symbolism, and pointed with pious morals) went straight to my heart; and though I skipped many of the fish chapters, I re-read many of the others, and 'The Complete Angler' did not a little to feed my strong natural love for out-door life and country pleasures, to confirm my habit of early rising, and to strengthen my attachment to the neighbourhood of a river.

"But my father's library furnished another volume for my garden studies. From him I inherited some of that taste which finds a magic attraction in dictionaries and grammars; and I only wish that I had properly mastered about half the languages in which it was the delight of my girlhood to dabble. As yet, however, I only looked at the 'grammar corner' with ambitious eyes, till one day there came upon me the desire to learn Russian. I asked my father for a Russian grammar, and he pointed out the only one that he possessed. My father seldom refused to lend us his books, and made no inquiries as to why we wanted them; but he was intensely strict about their proper treatment, so that we early learnt to turn over leaves from the top, to avoid dogs' ears, and generally to treat books properly and put them away punctually. Thus I got the grammar, and carried it off to the swing. Alas! it was not even Russian and English. It was a fat old French edition, interleaved for notes. The notes were my father's, and in English, which was of some assistance, and I set myself resolutely to learn the alphabet. But my progress was slow, and at last I got my father to write *Reka Dom* for me in Russian character, as I had determined to master these few letters first and then proceed. I soon became familiar with them, and was not a little proud of the achievement. I made a large copy to fasten upon the nursery wall; I wrote it in all my books; and Fatima, who could not be induced to attack the fat grammar with me, became equally absorbed on her part in the effort to reduce the inscription to cross-stitch for the benefit of her sampler.

"I borrowed the fat grammar again, and, in spite of my father's warnings that it was too difficult for me as yet, I hoped soon to be proficient in the language of the little Russians. But warnings from one's elders are apt to come true, and after a few vain efforts I left the tough old volume in its corner and took to easier pastimes.

"I had always an inventive turn, and was, as a rule, the director-in-chief of our amusements. I know I was often very tiresome and tyrannical in the ensuing arrangements, and can only hope the trouble I took on these occasions on behalf of my brothers and sisters, served in their eyes to balance my defects. I remember one device of mine that proved particularly troublesome.

"When sham battles had ended in real quarrels, and following in the footsteps of the little Russians was becoming irksome—(especially to Fatima, whose predecessor—Peter—had been of a military turn, and had begun fortifications near the kitchen garden which she was incompetent to carry out) a new idea struck me. I announced that letters properly written and addressed to the little Russians, 'Reka Dom, Russia,' and posted in the old rhubarb-pot by the tool-house, would be duly answered. The replies to be found in a week's time at the same office.

"The announcement was received with delight, and no doubt was ever expressed as to the genuineness of the answers which I regularly supplied, written, by the by, in excellent English, but with Reka Dom neatly effected in Russian characters on the note-paper. In the first place, I allowed no awkward inquiries into the machinery of my little plots for the benefit of the rest; and in the second, we had all, I think, a sort of half-and-half belief, a wilful credulity in reference to our many fancies (such as fairies and the like), of which it is impossible to give the exact measure. But when, the six weekly letters having become rather burdensome, I left off writing answers from Ivan to myself, the others began to inquire why Ivan never wrote now. As usual, I refused to give any explanations, and after inventing several for themselves which answered for awhile, they adopted by general consent an idea put forth by little Phillis. The child was sitting one day with her fat cheek on her hand, and her eyes on the rhubarb-pot, waiting for her share of the correspondence to be read aloud to her, when the fancy seemed to strike her, and she said quietly, but with an air of full conviction—

"'*I* know what it is—*Ivan is dead.*'"

"The idea took strange hold of us all. We said, 'Perhaps he is dead,' and spoke and thought of him as dead, till I think we were fully persuaded of it. No chair was set for him at the dolls' feasts, and I gained a sort of melancholy distinction as being without a partner now. 'You know Mary has no little Russian, since Ivan is dead.'"

"When our visible pets died, we buried them with much pomp, to the sound of a drum and a tin trumpet, in a piece of ground by the cabbage-bed; but in the present instance that ceremony was impossible. We resolved, however, to erect a gravestone to the memory of our fancy friend in his own garden. I had seen letters cut on stone, and was confident that with a chisel and hammer nothing could be easier. These the nursery tool-box furnished. I wrote out an elaborate inscription headed by Reka Dom in Russian characters, and we got a stone and set to work. The task, however, was harder than we had supposed. My long composition was discarded, and we resolved to be content with this simple sentence, *To the memory of Ivan.* But 'brevity is the soul of wit,' and the TO took so long to cut, that we threw out three more words, and the epitaph finally stood thus:

TO IVAN.

"In a rude fashion this was accomplished; and with crape on our arms and the accustomed music we set up the stone among the lilies."

* * * * *

"In time, Ida, we grew up, as it is called. Almost before we knew it, and whilst we still seemed to be looking forward to our emancipation from nursery authority and childish frocks, Fatima and I found ourselves grown-up young ladies, free to fashion our costume to our own tastes, and far from Reka Dom. Yes, we had changed our home again. The River House was ours no longer. Childhood also had slipped from our grasp, but slowly as the years had seemed to pass, they had not sufficed to accomplish every project we had made in them. Not one of those long summers by the river had seen that gorgeous display of flowers in our garden which in all good faith and energy we planned with every spring. I had not learnt Russian. Years had gone by since I first took up the fat grammar, but I had acquired little since that time beyond the familiar characters of the well-beloved name, Reka Dom.

"The country town that circumstances had now made our home possessed at least one attraction for us. It was here that our old friends the Misses Brooke had settled when their brother's death broke up the quiet little household. I was very fond of the good ladies; not less so now than I had been as a child, when their home-made buns and faded albums made an evening festive, and were looked forward to as a treat. They were good women, severe to themselves and charitable to others, who cultivated the grace of humility almost in excess. One little weakness, however, in their otherwise estimable characters had at times disturbed the even course of our friendship. I hardly know what to call it. It was not want of candour. More truthful women do not exist than they were, and I believe they never wilfully deceived anyone. I can only describe it as a habit of indulging in small plots and suspicions; a want of trust in other people, partly traceable, perhaps, to a lack of due confidence in themselves, but which was very provoking to one as young, eager, and sincerely affectionate as I was. I was indignant to discover little plots laid to test my sincerity; and to find my genuine (if not minutely measured) expressions of feeling doubted. If this peculiarity had been troublesome in the early stages of our acquaintance, it was doubly so when we met again, after the lapse of some years. For one thing, the dear ladies were older, and fidgety, foolish little weaknesses of this kind sometimes increase with years. Then I was older also, and if they had doubted their own powers of entertainment when I was a child, they would still less believe that I could enjoy their society now that I was a 'young lady.' Whereas the truth was, that though my taste for buns and my reverence for smooth pencil drawings in impossible perspective had certainly diminished, my real enjoyment of a quiet evening with my old friends was greater than before. I liked to take my sewing to their undisturbed fireside, and not a few pieces of work which had flagged under constant interruptions at home were rapidly finished as I chatted with them. I liked to draw out the acquirements which they would not believe that they possessed. I enjoyed rubbing my modern and desultory reading against their old-fashioned but solid knowledge. I admired their high and delicate principles, and respected their almost fatiguing modesty. At an age when religious questions move and often seriously trouble girls' minds, I drew comfort from their piety, which (although as quiet and modest as all their other virtues) had been for years, under my eyes, the ruling principle of all they did, the only subject on which they had the courage to speak with decision, the crown of their affections and pleasures, and the sufficient consolation of their sorrow. In addition to all this, when I went to them, I knew that my visit gave pleasure.

"It seemed hard that they could not always repose a similar confidence in me. And yet so it was. The consistent affection of years had failed to convince them that 'a young, pretty, lively girl' (as they were pleased to call me) could find pleasure in the society of 'two dull old women.' So they were apt to suspect either a second motive for my visit, or affectation in my appearance of enjoyment. At times I was chafed almost beyond my powers of endurance by these fancies; and on one occasion my vexation broke all bounds of respect.

"'You think me uncandid, ma'am,' I cried; 'and what are you? If you were to hear that I had spoken of you, elsewhere, as two dull old women, you would be as much astonished as angered. You know you would. You know you don't think I think so. I can't imagine why you say it!'"

"And my feelings being as much in the way of my logic as those of most other women, I got no further, but broke down into tears."

"'She says we're uncandid, Mary' sobbed Miss Martha."

"'So we are, I believe,' said Miss Mary, and then we all cried together."

"I think the protracted worry of this misunderstanding (which had been a long one) had made me almost hysterical. I clearly remember the feeling of lying with my face against the horsehair sofa in the little dining-room, feebly repeating, 'You shouldn't, you know. You shouldn't!' amid my tears, my hair being softly stroked the while by the two sisters, who comforted me, and blamed themselves with a depth of self-abasement that almost made me laugh. It had hardly seemed possible that their customary humility could go lower. The affair was wound up with a good deal of kissing, and tea, and there were no more suspicions for a long time.

* * * * *

"There had been peace, as I said, for long. But as, at the best of times, the Misses Brooke never gave us an invitation without going through the form of apologizing for the probable dulness of the entertainment, I was not surprised one morning to find myself invited to tea at Belle Vue Cottage for the following evening, on the strict condition that I should refuse the invitation if I felt disinclined to go. I had met the good ladies as we came out of church. There was Morning Prayer on Wednesdays and Fridays at one church in the town, and if the two little straw bonnets of the Misses Brooke had not been seen bending side by side at every service, the rest of the scanty congregation would have been as much astonished as if every one in the town who had time and opportunity for public worship had availed themselves of the privilege. On this day they had been there as usual, and when we turned up the street together, the invitation was given.

"'And could you induce your respected father to come with you, Mary dear?' added Miss Mary. 'You know our rooms are small, or we should be so glad to see Fatima. But we have a few friends coming, and she will understand.'"

"'Only a few,' Miss Martha said, hastily. 'Don't make her think there's anything worth coming for, Mary. And mind, Mary dear, if you don't care to come, that you say so. There's no need for "excuses" with us. And you know exactly what our tea-parties are.'"

"'Now, Miss Martha,' I said, shaking my fist at her, 'I won't bear it!'"

"'Well, my dear, you know it's true. And if you should have an invitation to the Lodge between now and to-morrow night, mind you throw us over. There's no dancing and heavy supper at the Cottage.'"

"'I'll eat a pound of beefsteak and have a private hornpipe to fortify me before I come, ma'am. And if the Lightfoots should ask me between now and then, I'll think about throwing over my oldest friends to oblige you!'"

"'You're very clever, my dear,' sighed Miss Martha, 'and it's easy to laugh at a stupid old woman like me.'"

"Now this was rather unfair, for I had only taken to banter on these occasions because a serious treatment of the subject had failed. I made my peace, however, by grave and affectionate assurances that I wished to come, and would like to come; and by adding a solemn promise that if I felt averse from it when the time came, I would stay at home.

"I was vexed to find symptoms of the old misunderstanding arising. The good ladies were evidently in a fidgety humour to-day, and going home full of it, I poured out my vexation to Fatima.

"Fatima's composure was not so easily ruffled as mine. She was apt to sit in easy, graceful attitudes, looking very idle, but getting through a wonderful amount of exquisite needlework, and listening to my passing grievances without being much disturbed herself.

"'I don't think I would worry myself,' she said, as she rapidly sorted the greens for a leaf in her embroidery. 'My idea is, that you will find the party more lively than usual. I have often noticed that when the old ladies are particularly full of apologies, something or somebody is expected.'"

"'I didn't want anything or anybody,' I said, dolefully; 'but I wish they wouldn't take fancies, and I wish they wouldn't put one through such cross-examinations about nothing. As to the party, who could there be, but the old set?'"

"'Nobody, I suppose. There'll be the Wilkinsons, of course;' and Fatima marked the fact with an emphatic stitch. 'And Mr. Ward, I suppose, and Dr. Brown, and the Jones's girls, and—'"

"'Oh, the rooms wouldn't hold more!' I said."

"'There's always room for one more—for a gentleman at any rate; and, depend upon it, it is as I say.'"

"Fatima was not so fond of the Misses Brooke as I was. She did not scruple to complain of the trouble it cost to maintain intimate relations with the excellent but touchy old ladies, and of the hot water about trifles into which one must perpetually fall.

"'I hope I am pretty trustworthy,' she would say, 'and I am sure you are, Mary. And if we are not, let them drop our acquaintance. But they treat their friends as we used to treat our flowers at Reka Dom! They are always taking them up to see how they are going on, and I like to vegetate in peace.'"

"I could not have criticized my dear and respected old friends so freely; but yet I knew that Fatima only spoke the truth."

"The subject was unexpectedly renewed at dinner."

"'Mary,' said my father, 'is there any mystery connected with this tea-party at Miss Brooke's?'"

"Fatima gave me a mischievous glance."

"'If there is, sir,' said I, 'I am not in the secret.'"

"'I met them in the town,' he went on, 'and they were good enough to invite me; and as I must see Ward about some registers, I ventured to ask if he were to be of the party (thinking to save my old legs a walk to his place). The matter was simple enough, but Miss Martha seemed to fancy that I wanted to know who was going to be there. I fully explained my real object, but either she did not hear or she did not believe me, I suppose, for she gave me a list of the expected company.'"

"'I am sure she would have believed you, sir, if she had realized what you were saying,' I said. 'I know the sort of thing, but I think that they are generally so absorbed in their own efforts to do what they think you want, they have no spare attention for what you say.'"

"'A very ingenious bit of special pleading, my dear, but you have not heard all. I had made my best bow and was just turning away, when Miss Martha, begging me to excuse her, asked with a good deal of mystery and agitation if *you* had commissioned me to find out who was to be at the party. I said I had not seen you since breakfast, but that I was quite able to assure her that if you had wished to find out anything on the subject, you would have gone direct to herself, with which I repeated my best bow in my best style, and escaped.'"

"I was too much hurt to speak, and Fatima took up the conversation with my father."

"'You will go, sir?' she said."

"'Of course, my dear, if Mary wishes it. Besides, Ward *is* to be there. I learnt so much.'"

"'You learnt more, sir,' said Fatima, 'and please don't leave us to die of curiosity. Who is to be there, after all?'"

"'The Wilkinsons, and Miss Jones and her sister, and Ward, and an old friend of Miss Brooke's, a merchant.'"

"'But his name, please!' cried Fatima, for my father was retreating to his study."

"'Smith—John Smith,' he answered laughing, and we were left alone."

"I was very much disposed to be injured and gloomy, but Fatima would not allow it. She was a very successful comforter. In the first place, she was thoroughly sympathetic; and in the second, she had a great dislike to any disturbance of the general peace and harmony, and at last, her own easy, cheerful view of things became infectious where no very serious troubles were concerned.

"'People must have their little weaknesses,' she said, 'and I am sure they haven't many failings.'"

"'This weakness is so unworthy of them,' I complained."

"'All good people's weaknesses are unworthy of them, my dear. And the better they are, the more unworthy the weakness appears. Now, Mary, do be reasonable! You know at the bottom how true they are, and how fond of you. Pray allow them a few fidgety fancies, poor old dears. No doubt we shall be just as fidgety when we are as old. I'm sure I shall have as many fancies as hairs in my wig, and as to you, considering how little things weigh on your mind now—'"

"Fatima's reasoning was not conclusive, but I think I came at last to believe that Miss Brooke's distrust was creditable to herself, and complimentary to me—so it certainly must have been convincing.

"'And now,' she concluded, 'come upstairs and forget it. For I have got two new ideas on which I want your opinion. The first is a new stitch, in which I purpose to work some muslin dresses for us both. I thought of it in bed this morning. The second is a new plan for braiding your hair, which came into my head whilst father was reading aloud that speech to us last night. I had just fastened up the last plait when he laid down the paper.'"

"'You absurd Fatima!' I cried. 'How could you! And it was so interesting!'"

"'Don't look shocked,' said Fatima. 'I shall never be a politician. Of all studies, that of politics seems to me the most disturbing and uncomfortable. If some angel, or inspired person would tell me which side was in the right, and whom to believe in, I could be a capital partisan. As it is, I don't worry myself with it; and last night when you were looking flushed and excited at the end of the speech, I was calmly happy—"'

"'But, Fatima,' I broke in, 'you don't mean to say—"'

"'If it had lasted five minutes longer,' said Fatima, 'I should have comfortably decided whether ferns or ivy would combine better with the loops.'"

"'But, Fatima! were you really not listening when—'"

"'On the whole I decide for ivy,' said Fatima, and danced out of the room, I following and attempting one more remonstrance in the hall."

"'But, Fatima!—'"

"'With perhaps a suspicion of white chrysanthemums,' she added over the banisters."

"Both the new ideas promised to be successful, and the following evening my hair was dressed in what Fatima now called the political plaits. From the first evening of my introduction into society she had established herself as my lady's maid. She took a generous delight in dressing me up, and was as clever as she was kind about it. This evening she seemed to have surpassed herself, as I judged by the admiring exclamations of our younger sister Phillis—a good little maid, who stood behind my chair with combs and pins in her hand as Fatima's aide-de-camp. Finally, the dexterous fingers interwove some sprays of ivy with the hair, and added white rosebuds for lack of chrysanthemums.

"'Perfect!' Fatima exclaimed, stepping backwards with gestures of admiration that were provokingly visible in the glass before which I sat. 'And to think that it should be wasted on an uninteresting tea-party! You will not wear your new muslin, of course?'"

"'Indeed, I shall,' I answered. 'You know I always make myself smart for the Cottage.' Which was true, and my reason for it was this. I had once gone there to a quiet tea-party in a dress that was rather too smart for the occasion, and which looked doubly gay by contrast with the sombre costume of the elderly friends whom I met. I was feeling vexed with myself for an error in taste, when Miss Mary came up to me, and laying her hands affectionately on me, and smoothing my ribbons, thanked me for having come in such a pretty costume.

"'You come in, my dear,' she said, 'like a fresh nosegay after winter. You see we are old women, my love, and dress mostly in black, since dear James's death; and our friends are chiefly elderly and sombre-looking also. So it is a great treat to us to look at something young and pretty, and remember when we were girls, and took pains with such things ourselves.'"

"'I was afraid I was too smart, Miss Mary,' I said."

"'To be sure it is a waste to wear your pretty things here,' Miss Mary added; 'but you might let us know sometimes when you are going to a grand party, and we will come and look at you.'"

"I was touched by the humble little lady's speech, and by the thought of how little one is apt to realize the fact that faded, fretful, trouble-worn people in middle life have been young, and remember their youth.

"Thenceforward I made careful toilettes for the Cottage, and this night was not an exception to the rule."

"I was dressed early; my father was rather late, and we three girls had nearly an hour's chat before I had to go."

"We began to discuss the merchant who was to vary the monotony of our small social circle. Phillis had heard that a strange gentleman had arrived in the town this afternoon by the London stage. Fatima had an idea on the subject which she boldly stated. One of the Misses Brooke was going to be married—to this London merchant. We were just at an age when a real life romance is very attractive, and the town was not rich in romances—at least, in our little society. So Fatima's idea found great favour with us, and, as she described it, seemed really probable. Here was an old friend, a friend of their youth, and probably a lover, turned up again, and the sisters were in a natural state of agitation. (It fully accounted for Miss Martha's suspicious sensitiveness yesterday, and I felt ashamed of having being aggrieved.) Doubtless the lovers had not been allowed to marry in early life because he was poor. They had been parted, but had remained faithful. He had made a fortune, like Dick Whittington, and now, a rich London merchant, had come back to take his old love home. Being an old friend, it was obviously a youthful attachment; and being a merchant, he must be very rich. This happy combination—universal in fiction, though not invariable in real life—was all that could be desired, and received strong confirmation from the fact of his coming from London; for in those days country girls seldom visited the metropolis, and we regarded the great city with awe, as the centre of all that was wealthy and wonderful. It was a charming story, and though we could not but wish that he had returned before Miss Martha took to a 'front' and spectacles, yet we pictured a comfortable domestic future for them; and Fatima was positive that 'worlds' might be done for the appearance of the future Mrs. Smith by more tasteful costume, and longed ardently to assume the direction of her toilette.

"'I don't believe that she need wear a front,' she pleaded. 'I daresay she has plenty of pretty grey hair underneath. Spectacles are intellectual, if properly worn; which, by the by, they need not be at meals when your husband is looking at you across the table; and as to caps—'"

"But here my father knocked at the door, and I put on my cloak and hood, and went with him."

"The Misses Brooke received us affectionately, but I thought with some excitement, and a flush on Miss Martha's cheeks almost made me smile. I could not keep Fatima's fancy out of my head. Indeed, I was picturing my old friend in more cheerful and matronly costume presiding over the elegant belongings of a stout, well-to-do, comfortable Mr. John Smith, as I moved about in the little room, and exchanged mechanical smiles and greetings with the familiar guests. I had settled the sober couple by their fireside, and was hesitating between dove-colour and lavender-grey for the wedding silk, when Miss Martha herself disturbed me before I had decided the important question. I fancied a slight tremor in her voice as she said—

"'Mr. John Smith.'"

"I dropped a more formal curtsey than I had hitherto done, as was due to a stranger and a gentleman, and looked once at the object of my benevolent fancies, and then down again at my mittens. His head was just coming up from a low bow, and my instantaneous impression was, 'He wears a brown wig.' But in a moment more he was upright, and I saw that he did not. And—he certainly was not suitable in point of age. I took one more glance to make sure, and meeting his eyes, turned hastily, and plunged into conversation with my nearest neighbour, not noticing at the instant who it was. As I recovered from my momentary confusion, I became aware that I was talking to the rector's wife, and had advanced some opinions on the subject of the weather which she was energetically disputing. I yielded gracefully, and went back to my thoughts. I hope Miss Martha did not feel as I did the loss of that suitable, comfortable, middle-aged partner my fancy had provided for her. It did seem a pity that he had no existence. I thought that probably marriage was the happiest condition for most people, and felt inclined to discuss the question with the rector's wife, who had had about twenty-two years' exemplary experience of that state. Then I should like to have helped to choose the silk—

"At this point I was asked to play."

"I played some favourite things of Miss Brooke's and some of my own, Mr. Smith turning over the leaves of my music; and then he was asked to sing, and to my astonishment, prepared to accompany himself. Few English gentlemen (if any) could accompany their own songs on the pianoforte in my youth, Ida; most of them then had a wise idea that the pianoforte was an instrument 'only fit for women,' and would have as soon thought of trying to learn to play upon it as of studying the spinning-wheel. I do not know that I had ever heard one play except my father, who had lived much abroad. When Mr. Smith sat down at the instrument, I withdrew into a corner, where Miss Martha followed me as if to talk. But when he began, I think every one was silent.

"The song he sang is an old one now, Ida, but it was comparatively new then, and it so happened that very few of us had heard it before. It was 'Home, Sweet Home.' He had a charming voice, with a sweet pathetic ring about it, and his singing would have redeemed a song of far smaller merit, and of sentiment less common to all his hearers. As it was, our sympathies were taken by storm. The rector's wife sobbed audibly, but, I believe, happily, with an oblique reference to the ten children she had left at home; and poor Miss Martha, behind me, touched away tear after tear with her thin finger-tips, and finally took to her pocket-handkerchief, and thoughts of the dear dead brother, and the little house and garden, and I know not what earlier home still. As for me, I thought of Reka Dom.

"We had had many homes, but that was *the* home *par excellence*—the beloved of my father, the beloved of us all. And as the clear voice sang the refrain, which sounded in some of our ears like a tender cry of recall to past happiness,

'Home—Home—sweet, sweet Home!'"

I stroked Miss Martha's knee in silent sympathy, and saw Reka Dom before my eyes. The river seemed to flow with the melody. I swung to the tune between the elm-trees, with Walton and Cotton on my lap. What would Piscator have thought of it, had the milkmaid sung him this song? I roamed through the three lawns that were better to me than pleasures and palaces, and stood among the box-edged gardens. Then the refrain called me back again—

'Home—Home—sweet, sweet Home!'"

I was almost glad that it ended before I, too, quite broke down.

"Everybody crowded round the singer with admiration of the song, and inquiries about it."

"'I heard it at a concert in town the other day,' he said, 'and it struck me as pretty, so I got a copy. It is from an English opera called "Clari," and seems the only pretty thing in it.'"

"'Do you not like it?' Miss Jones asked me; I suppose because I had not spoken."

"'I think it is lovely,' I said, 'as far as I can judge; but it carries one away from criticism; I do not think I was thinking of the music; I was thinking of Home.'"

"'Exactly.'"

"It was not Miss Jones who said 'Exactly,' but the merchant, who was standing by her; and he said it, not in that indefinite tone of polite assent with which people commonly smile answers to each other's remarks at evening parties, but as if he understood the words from having thought the thought. We three fell into conversation about the song—about 'Clari'—about the opera—the theatre—about London; and then Dr. Brown, who had been educated in the great city, joined us, and finally he and Miss Jones took the London subject to themselves, and the merchant continued to talk to me. He was very pleasant company, chiefly from being so alive with intelligence that it was much less trouble to talk with him than with any one I had ever met, except my father. He required so much less than the average amount of explanation. It hardly seemed possible to use too few words for him to seize your meaning by both ends, so to speak; the root your idea sprang from, and conclusion to which it tended.

"We talked of music—of singing—of the new song, and of the subject of it—home. And so of home-love, and patriotism, and the characters of nations in which the feeling seemed to predominate.

"'Like everything else, it depends partly on circumstances, I suppose,' he said. 'I sometimes envy people who have only one home—the eldest son of a landed proprietor, for instance. I fancy I have as much home-love in me as most people, but it has been divided; I have had more homes than one.'"

"'*I* have had more homes than one,' I said; 'but with me I do not think it has been divided. At least, one of the homes has been so much dearer than the others.'"

"'Do you not think so because it is the latest, and your feelings about it are freshest?' he asked."

"I laughed. 'A bad guess. It is not my present home. This one was near a river.'"

"'Exactly.'"

"This time the 'exactly' did not seem so appropriate as before, and I explained further."

"'For one thing we were there when I was at an age when attachment to a place gets most deeply rooted, I think. As a mere child one enjoys and suffers like a kitten from hour to hour. But when one is just old enough to form associations and weave dreams, and yet is still a child—it is then, I fancy, that a home gets almost bound up with one's life.'"

"He simply said 'Yes,' and I went on. Why, I can hardly tell, except that to talk on any subject beyond mere current chit-chit, and be understood, was a luxury we did not often taste at the tea-parties of the town.

"'And yet I don't know if my theory will hold good, even in our case,' I went on, 'for my father was quite as much

Juliana Horatia Ewing

devoted to the place as we were, and fell in love with it quite as early. But the foreign name was the first attraction to him, I think."'

"'It was abroad, then?' he asked."

"I explained, and again I can hardly tell why, but I went on talking till I had given him nearly as full a history of Reka Dom as I have given to you. For one thing he seemed amazingly interested in the recital, and drew out many particulars by questions; and then the song had filled my head with tender memories, and happy little details of old times, and it was always pleasant to prose about the River Home, as indeed, my child, it is pleasant still.

"We were laughing over some childish reminiscence, when Miss Martha tapped me on the shoulder and said rather louder than usual—

"'Dear Mary, there are some engravings here, my love, I should like you to look at.'"

"I felt rather astonished, for I knew every book and picture in the house as well as I knew my own, but I followed her to a table, when she added, in a fluttering whisper—

"'You'll excuse my interrupting you, my love, I'm sure; but it was becoming quite particular.'"

"I blushed redder than the crimson silk binding of the 'Keepsake' before me. I wished I could honestly have misunderstood Miss Martha's meaning. But I could not. Had I indeed talked too much and too long to a gentleman and a stranger? (It startled me to reflect how rapidly we had passed that stage of civil commonplace which was the normal condition of my intercourse with the gentlemen of the town.)

I was certainly innocent of any intentional transgression of those bounds of reticence and decorum which are a young lady's best friends, but as to the length of my conversation with the merchant I felt quite uncertain and unspeakably alarmed.

"I was indulging a few hasty and dismal reflections when Miss Martha continued—

"'When I was young, dear Mary, I remember a valuable piece of advice that was given me by my excellent friend and schoolmistress, Miss Peckham, "If you are only slightly acquainted with a gentleman, talk of indifferent matters. If you wish to be friendly but not conspicuous, talk of *his* affairs; but only if you mean to be very intimate, speak of yourself;'" and adding, 'I'm sure you'll forgive me, my love,' Miss Martha fluttered from the table.

"At the moment I was feeling provoked both with her and with myself, and did not feel so sure about the forgiveness as she professed to be; but of one thing I felt perfectly certain. Nothing but sheer necessity should induce me to speak another syllable to the London merchant.

"Circumstances did not altogether favour my resolution. I scrupulously avoided so much as a look at Mr. Smith, though in some mysterious way I became conscious that he and my father were having a long *tete-a-tete* conversation in a corner. I devoted myself exclusively to the rector's wife till supper, and then I carefully chose the opposite side of the table to that to which the merchant seemed to be going. But when I was fairly seated, for some reason he gave up his place to someone else, and when it was impossible for me to change my seat, he took the one next to it. It was provoking, but I steadily resisted his attempts to talk, and kept my face as much averted as possible. Once or twice he helped me to

Juliana Horatia Ewing

something on the table, but I barely thanked him, and never lifted my eyes to his face. I could not, however, avoid seeing the hand that helped me, and idly noticing a ring that I had remarked before, when he was playing. It was a fine blue stone, a lapis lazuli, curiously and artistically set. 'Rich merchants can afford such baubles!' I thought. It was very tasteful, however, and did not look like English work. There was something engraven upon it, which did not look like English either. Was it Greek? I glanced at it with some curiosity, for it reminded me of—but that was nonsense, a fancy that came because the subject was in my mind. At this moment the hand and ring were moved close to me and I looked again.

"It was not a fancy. There was no mistaking the inscription this time. I had learnt it too thoroughly—written it too often—loved it too well—it was *Reka Dom*.

"For a moment I sat in blind astonishment. Then the truth suddenly flashed upon me. The merchant's name was the name of our predecessors at Reka Dom. True, it was such a common one that I had met more than one family of Smiths since then without dreaming of any connection between them and the River House. And yet, of course, it was there that the Misses Brooke had known him. Before our time. Which could he be? He was too young to be the father, and there was no John among the little Russians—unless, yes, it was the English version of one of the Russian names—and this was Ivan.

"It crowned my misfortunes. What would Miss Martha say if she knew what had been the subject of our conversation? Would that that excellent rule which had been the guide of her young ladyhood had curtailed the conversational propensities of mine! I thought of the three degrees of intimacy with a shudder. Why had we not been satisfied with discussing the merits of the song?

"We had gone on to talk of him and his homes, and as if that were not enough, had proceeded further to me and mine. I got red as I sat listening to some civil chat from Mr. Ward the curate (eminently in the most innocent stage of the first degree), and trying to recall what we had not spoken of in connection with that Home which had been so beloved of both of us, and that Ivan whose lilies I had tended for years.

"I grew nearly frantic as I thought that he must think that I had known who he was, and wildly indignant with the fancy for small mysteries which had kept Miss Brooke from telling us whom we were going to meet."

"At last the evening came to an end. I was cloaking myself in the hall when the merchant came up and offered his help, which I declined. But he did not go, and stood so that I could not help seeing a distressed look in his eyes, and the nervous way in which he was turning the blue ring upon his finger.

"'I have so wanted to speak to you again,' he said. 'I wanted to say—'"

"But at this moment I caught Miss Martha's eye in the parlour doorway, and, dropping a hasty curtsey, I ran to my father."

"'A very nice young fellow,' my father observed, as I took his arm outside; 'a superior, sensible, well informed gentleman, such as you don't meet with every day.'"

"I felt quite unequal to answering the remark, and he went on:

"'What funny little ways your old friends have, my dear, to

Juliana Horatia Ewing

be sure. Considering how few strangers come to the place, it would have been natural for them to tell us all about the one they asked us to meet; and as they had known both him and us, as tenants of Reka Dom, it was doubly natural that they should speak of him to us, and of us to him. But he told me that we were just the people present of whom he had not heard a word. He seems both fond of them and to appreciate their little oddities. He told me he remembers, as a boy, that they never would call him Ivan, which is as much his name as any by which a man was ever baptized. They thought it might give him a tendency to affectation to bear so singular a name in England. They always called him John, and keep up the discipline still. When he arrived yesterday they expressed themselves highly satisfied with the general improvement in him, and he said he could hardly help laughing as Miss Martha added, 'And you seem to have quite shaken off that little habit of affectation which—you'll excuse me, dear John—you had as a boy.' He says that, to the best of his belief, his only approach to affectation consisted in his being rather absent and ungainly, and in a strong aversion from Mr. Brooke.'"

"'Did the old gentleman wear that frightful shade in his time?' I asked."

"'Not always,' he says, 'but he looked worse without it. He told me a good deal about him that I had never heard. He remembered hearing it spoken of as a boy. It appears that the brother was very wild and extravagant in his youth; drank, too, I fancy, and gave his poor sisters a world of trouble, after breaking the heart of the widowed mother who had spoiled him. When she died the sisters lived together, and never faltered in their efforts to save him—never shut their doors against him when he would return—and paid his debts over and over again. He spent all his own fortune, and most of theirs, besides being the means of breaking off comfortable marriages for both. Mr. Smith thinks that a long illness checked his career, and eventually he reformed."'

"'I hope he was grateful to his poor sisters,' I said."

"'One naturally thinks that he must have been so, but Smith's remark was very just. He said, "I fancy he was both penitent and grateful as far as he was able, but I believe he had been too long accustomed to their unqualified self-sacrifice to feel it very sensitively!" And I believe he is right. Such men not seldom reform in conduct if they live long enough, but few eyes that have been blinded by years of selfishness are opened to see clearly in this world."'

"'It ought to make one very tender with the good ladies' little weaknesses,' I said, self-reproachfully; and I walked home in a more peaceful state of mind. I forgave poor Miss Martha; also I was secretly satisfied that my father had found the merchant's conversation attractive. It seemed to give me some excuse for my breach of Miss Peckham's golden rule. Moreover, little troubles and offences which seemed mountains at Bellevue Cottage were apt to dwindle into very surmountable molehills with my larger-minded parents. I was comparatively at ease again. My father had evidently seen nothing unusual in my conduct, so I hoped that it had not been conspicuous. Possibly I might never meet Mr. Smith any more. I rather hoped not. Life is long, and the world wide, and it is sometimes possible to lose sight of people with whom one has disagreeable associations. And then it was a wholesome lesson for the future.

"'And what was the old gentleman like?' was Fatima's first question, when I came upstairs. I had just been talking of Mr. Brooke, and no other old gentleman occurred to my memory at that moment.

"'What old gentleman?' I asked dreamily."

"'Miss Martha's old gentleman, the merchant—wasn't he there, after all?'"

"I blushed at my stupidity, and at a certain feeling of guiltiness in connection with the person alluded to."

"'Oh, yes, he was there,' I answered; 'but he is not an old gentleman.'"

"'What is he, then?' Fatima asked, curiously."

"It is undoubtedly a luxury to be the bearer of a piece of startling intelligence, and it is well not to spoil the enjoyment of it by over haste. I finished unsnapping my necklace, and said, very deliberately—

"'He is one of the little Russians.'"

"Fatima's wit jumped more quickly than mine had done. It was she who added—

"'Then he is Ivan.'"

* * * * *

"My hopes in reference to Mr. Smith were disappointed. I had not seen the last of him. My mother was at this time from home, and I was housekeeper in her absence. It was on the morning following the Bellevue tea-party that my father said to me—

"'Mr. Smith is coming up to refer to a book of mine to-day, my dear; and I asked him to stay to dinner. I suppose it will be convenient?'"

"I said, 'Certainly, sir.'"

"I could plead no domestic inconvenience; but I thought that Mr. Smith might have gone quietly back to London by the early coach, and spared me the agitation which the prospect of seeing him again undoubtedly excited. He came, however. It was the first visit, but by no means the last; and he lingered in the town, greatly to my father's satisfaction (who had taken a strong fancy for him), but not, apparently, to that of the Misses Brooke.

"As I afterwards found the clue to the somewhat strange conduct of our old friends at this time, I may as well briefly state how it was."

"When the merchant first announced to them his proposed business visit to the town, and his intention of calling on them, the good ladies (in their affection for me, and having a high opinion of him) planned a kindly little romance of which he and I were to be the hero and heroine, and which was to end in our happy marriage. With this view they arranged for our meeting at the tea-party, and avoided all mention of each to the other, that we might meet in the (so to speak) incidental way characteristic of real love stories. With that suspiciousness of people in general, and of young people in particular, which haunted Miss Martha, she attributed my ready acceptance of the invitation to my having heard of Mr. Smith's arrival, and to the unusual attraction of an eligible gentleman at the tea-party. Little did she guess the benevolent plans which on my part I had formed for her, and which the merchant's youthful appearance had dashed to the ground.

"It is sometimes the case, my dear Ida, that people who make these kind plans for their friends, become dissatisfied with the success of their arrangements if they themselves cease to be the good genii of the plot. If, that is, matters seem likely to fall out as they wish, but without their assistance. It was so with the Misses Brooke, and especially with Miss Martha. Fully aware of the end which she in her own mind proposed to our acquaintance, my long conversation with the merchant struck her as an indelicate readiness to accept attentions which had matrimony in her perspective, and which she had designed to be the gradual result of sundry well-chaperoned and studiously incidental interviews at the Cottage. And when, so far from thankfully accepting these incidental meetings, the merchant took upon himself to become an almost daily visitor at our house, and delayed his return to London far beyond the time proposed for his departure, the good lady's view underwent a decided change. It was 'a pity' that a young man like John Smith should neglect his business. It was also 'a pity' that dear Mary's mother was not at home. And when I took occasion casually to allude to the fact that Mr. Smith's visits were paid to my father, and (with the exception of an occasional meal) were passed in the study amongst German pamphlets, my statement was met by kind, incredulous smiles, and supplemented with general and somewhat irritating observations on the proper line of conduct for young ladies at certain crises of life. Nothing could be kinder than Miss Martha's intentions, and her advice might have been a still greater kindness if she would have spoken straight-forwardly, and believed what I said. As it was, I left off going to Bellevue Cottage, and ardently wished that the merchant would go back to his merchandise, and leave our quiet little town to its own dull peace.

"Sometimes I thought of the full-grown man whose intelligent face, and the faintly foreign accent of whose voice were now familiar in our home—the busy merchant, the polite and agreeable gentleman. And then I thought of the Ivan I seemed to have known so much better so long ago! The pale boy wandering by the water—reading in the swing—dead by that other river—buried beneath the lilies.

Oh! why had he lived to come back in this new form to trouble me?

"One day he came to my father as usual, and I took the opportunity to call on my old friends. I felt ashamed of having neglected them, and as I knew that Mr. Smith was at our house, I could not be suspected of having hoped to meet him at theirs. But I called at an unfortunate moment. Miss Martha had just made up her mind that in the absence of my mother, and the absentness of my father, it was the duty of old friends like herself to give me a little friendly counsel. As she took a great deal of credit for being 'quite candid, my dear,' and quietly, but persistently refused to give me credit for the same virtue, I was too much irritated to appreciate the kindness which led her to undertake the task of interference in so delicate a matter; and found her remarks far from palatable. In the midst of them the merchant was announced.

"If I could have looked innocent it would have done me no good. As it was, I believe I looked very guilty. After sitting for a few minutes longer I got up to go, when to my horror the merchant rose also. The old ladies made no effort to detain him, but Miss Martha's face spoke volumes as we left the house. Half mad with vexation, I could hardly help asking him why he was stupid enough to come away just at the moment I had chosen for leaving; but he forestalled the inquiry by a voluntary explanation. He wished to speak to me. He had something to say.

"When he had said it, and had asked me to marry him, my cup was full. I refused him with a vehemence which must have surprised him, modest as he was, and rushed wildly home.

"For the next few days I led a life of anything but comfort. First as to Ivan. My impetuous refusal did not satisfy him, and he wrote me a letter over which I shed bitter tears of indescribable feeling.

"Then as to my father. The whole affair took him by surprise. He was astonished, and very much put out, especially as my mother was away. So far from its having been, as with the Misses Brooke, the first thing to occur to him, he repeatedly and emphatically declared that it was the very last thing he should have expected. He could neither imagine what had made the merchant think of proposing to me, nor what had made me so ready to refuse him. Then they were in the very middle of a crabbed pamphlet, in which Ivan's superior knowledge of German had been invaluable. It was most inconvenient.

"'Why didn't I like poor Ivan?'"

"Ah, my child, did I not like him!"

"'Then why was I so cross to him?'"

"Indeed, Ida, I think the old ladies' 'ways' were chiefly to blame for this. Their well-meant but disastrous ways of making you feel that you were doing wrong, or in the wrong, over matters the most straight-forward and natural. But I was safe under the wing of my mother, before I saw Ivan again; and—many as were the years he and I were permitted to spend together—I think I may truthfully say that I was never cross to him any more.

"'What did he say in that letter that made me cry?'"

"He asked to be allowed to make himself better known to me, before I sent him quite away. And this developed an ingenious notion in my father's brain, that no better opportunity could, from every point of view, be found for this, than that I should be allowed to sit with them in the study whilst he and Ivan went on with the German pamphlet.

"The next call I paid at Bellevue Cottage was to announce my engagement, and I had some doubt of the reception my news might meet with. But I had no kinder or more loving congratulations than those of the two sisters. Small allusion was made to bygones. But when Miss Martha murmured in my ear—

"'You'll forgive my little fussiness and over-anxiety, dear Mary. One would be glad to guard one's young friends from some of the difficulties and disappointments one has known oneself—' I thought of the past life of the sisters, and returned her kiss with tenderness. Doubtless she had feared that the merchant might be trifling with my feelings, and that a thousand other ills might happen when the little love affair was no longer under her careful management. But all ending well, was well; and not even the Bellevue cats were more petted by the old ladies than we two were in our brief and sunny betrothal.

"Sunny, although for the most part it was winter time. When we would sit by the fireside in the privileged idleness of lovers, sometimes at home, sometimes in the Cottage parlour; and Ivan would tell of the Russian Reka Dom, and of all the winter beauties and pleasures of that other river which was for months a frozen highway, with gay sleighs flying, jingling over the snow roads, and peasants wrapped in sheepskin crossing from the country to market in the town. How dogs and children rolled together in snow so dry from intense cold that it hardly wet them more than sand. And how the river closed, and when it opened, with all the local traditions connected with these events; and of the stratagems resorted to to keep Jack Frost out of the houses, and of the stores laid up against the siege of the Winter King.

"But through the most interesting of his narratives Fatima's hands were never idle. She seemed to have concentrated all her love for me into those beautiful taper fingers, which laboured ceaselessly in exquisite needlework on my wedding clothes.

"And when the lilies of the valley were next in blossom, Ivan and I were married."

"The blue-stoned ring was cut down to fit my finger, and was, by my desire, my betrothal ring, and I gave Ivan another instead of it. Inside his was engraven the inscription we had cut upon his tombstone at Reka Dom,—

"'TO IVAN.'"

It was a long story, and Nurse had been waiting some little time in the old lady's kitchen when it came to an end.

"And is Ivan—?" Ida hesitatingly began.

"Dead. Many years since, my child," said the little old lady; "you need not be afraid to speak of him, my dear. All that is past. We used to hope that we should neither of us long outlive the other, but God willed it otherwise. It was very bitter at first, but it is different now. The days and hours that once seemed to widen our separation are now fast bringing us together again."

"Was he about papa's age when he died?" Ida gently asked.

"He was older than your father can have been, my love, I think. He was a more than middle-aged man. He died of fever. It was in London, but in his delirium he fancied that the river was running by the windows, and when I bathed his head he believed that the cooling drops were from the waters of his old home.'"

"Didn't he know you?" Ida asked, with sudden sympathy.

"He knew the touch of my hands always, my dear. It was my greatest comfort. That, and the short time of perfect reason before he sank to rest. We had been married thirty years, and I had worn my silver wedding-ring with even more pride than the golden one. There have been lilies on the grave of the true Ivan for half that time, and will be, perhaps, for yet a little while, till I also am laid beneath them.

"So ends the story, my dear," the little old lady added, after a pause.

"I should like to know what became of the old landlord, please," Ida said.

"If you will ask an old woman like me the further history of the people she knew in her youth," said Mrs. Overtheway, smiling, "you must expect to hear of deaths. Of course he is dead many a long year since. We became very intimate with him whilst we were his tenants, and, I believe, cheered the close of his life. He and my father were fast friends, but it was to my mother that he became especially devoted. He said she was an exception to her sex, which from his point of view was a high compliment. He had unbounded confidence in her judgment, and under her influence, eventually modified many of his peculiar habits. She persuaded him to allot a very moderate sum to housekeeping expenses, and to indulge in the economical luxury of a trustworthy servant. He consented to take into use a good suit of clothes which he possessed, and in these the old man was wont at last to accompany us to church, and to eat his Sunday dinner with us afterwards. I do not think he was an illiberal man at heart, but he had been very poor in his youth—('So poor, ma'am,'

Juliana Horatia Ewing

he said one day to my mother, 'that I could not live with honour and decency in the estate of a gentleman. I did not live. I starved—and bought books,')—and he seemed unable to shake off the pinching necessity of years. A wealthy uncle who had refused to help him whilst he lived, bequeathed all his money to him when he died. But when late in life the nephew became rich, habits of parsimony were a second nature, and seemed to have grown chronic and exaggerated under the novel anxieties of wealth. He still 'starved—and bought books.' During the last years of his life he consulted my mother (and, I fancy, other people also) on the merits of various public charities in the place and elsewhere; so that we were not astonished after his death to learn from his will that he had divided a large part of his fortune amongst charitable institutions. With the exception of a few trifling legacies to friends, the rest of his money was divided in equal and moderate bequests to relatives. He left some valuable books to my father, and the bulk of his library to the city where he was born."

"Was your mother with him when he died?" Ida asked.

"She was, my dear. But, sadly enough, only at the very last. We were at the seaside when he was seized by his last illness, and no one told us, for indeed it is probable that few people knew. At last a letter from the servant announced that he was dying, and had been most anxious to see my mother, and she hastened home. The servant seemed relieved by her arrival, for the old gentleman was not altogether an easy patient to nurse. He laughed at the doctor, she said, and wouldn't touch a drop of his medicine, but otherwise was as patient as a sick gentleman could be, and sat reading his Bible all the day long. It was on the bed when my mother found him, but his eyes were dimming fast. He held out his hands to my mother, and as she bent over him said something of which she could only catch three words—'the true riches.' He never spoke again."

"Poor man?" said Ida: "I think he was very nice. What became of his cat?"

"Dead—dead—dead!" said the little old lady; "Ida, my child, I will answer no more questions."

"One more, please," said Ida! "where is that dear, dear Fatima?"

"No, my child, no! Nothing more about her. Dear, dear Fatima, indeed! And yet I will just tell you that she married, and that her husband (older even than I am, and very deaf) is living still. He and I are very fond of each other, though, having been a handsome man he is sensitive about his personal appearance, and will not use a trumpet, which I consider weak. But we get on very well. He smells my flowers, and smiles and nods to me, and says something in a voice so low that I can't hear it; and I stick a posy in his buttonhole, and smile and nod to him, and say something in a voice so loud that *he* can't hear it; and so we go on. One day in each year we always spend together, and go to church. The first of November."

"That is—?" said Ida.

"The Feast of All Saints, my child."

"Won't you tell me any more?" Ida asked.

"No, my dear. Not now, at any rate. Remember I am old, and have outlived almost all of those I loved in my youth. It is right and natural that death should be sad in your eyes, my child, and I will not make a tragedy of the story of Reka Dom.

*   *   *   *   *

        Juliana Horatia Ewing

"Then your real name," said Ida, as she gave the old lady a farewell kiss, "is—"

"Mary Smith, my dear," said Mrs. Overtheway.

*   *   *   *   *

Next morning the little old lady went to church as usual, and Ida was at the window when she returned. When the child had seen her old friend into the house she still kept her place, for the postman was coming down the street, and it was amusing to watch him from door to door, and to see how large a bundle of letters he delivered at each. At Mrs. Overtheway's he delivered one, a big one, and an odd curiosity about this letter took possession of Ida. She wished she knew what it was about, and from whom it came, though, on the face of it, it was not likely she would be much the wiser if she did. She was still at the window when the door of the opposite house was opened, and the little old lady came hurriedly out. She had only her cap upon her head, and she held an open letter in her hand; *the* letter, it was evident. When she reached the little green gate she seemed to recollect herself, and, putting her hand to her head, went back into the house. Ida waited anxiously to see if she would come out again, and presently she appeared, this time in her bonnet, but still with the letter in her hand. She crossed the street, and seemed to be coming to the house. Then the bell rang, and in she came. Ida's curiosity became intense, and was not lessened by the fact that the little old lady did not come to her, but stayed below talking with some one. The old gentleman had not returned, so it must be Nurse.

At last the conversation came to an end, and Mrs. Overtheway came upstairs.

She kissed Ida very tenderly, and inquired after her health;

but though she seemed more affectionate than usual, Ida felt persuaded that something was the matter. She drew a chair to the fire, and the old lady sat down, saying—

"May I stay a little with you, my dear?"

"Oh, thank you?" said Ida, and put a footstool for the old lady's feet.

Mrs. Overtheway stroked her head tenderly for some time in silence, and then said, in a gentle voice—

"I have something to tell you, my dear."

"Another story?" Ida asked. "Oh, thank you, if it is another story."

The old lady was silent, but at last she said, as if to herself—

"Perhaps best so," and added: "yes, my love, I will tell you a story."

Ida thanked her warmly, and another pause ensued.

"I hardly know where to begin, or what to tell you of this story," said the little old lady at last, seeming to falter for the first time in her Scharazad-like powers of narration.

"Let it be about a Home, please; if you can," said Ida.

"A home!" said the old lady, and strangely enough, she seemed more agitated than when she had spoken of Reka Dom—"It should have begun with a broken home, but it shall not. It should end with a united home, God willing. A home! I must begin with a far-away one, a strange one, on the summit of high cliffs, the home of fearless, powerful

Juliana Horatia Ewing

creatures, white-winged like angels."

"It's a fairy tale," said Ida.

"No, my child, it is true."

"It sounds like a fairy tale," Ida said.

"It shall be a tale of that description, if you like," said the old lady, after a pause, "but, as I said, the main incidents are true."

"And the white-winged creatures?" Ida asked. "Were they fairies?"

"No, my love; birds. But if to see snowy albatrosses with their huge white wings wheeling in circles about a vessel sailing in mid ocean be anything like what I have read of and heard described, fairyland could hardly show anything more beautiful and impressive."

"Do they fly near ships, then?" Ida asked.

"Yes, my child. I remember my husband describing them to me as he had once seen them in southern seas. He said that when he saw them, great, white, and majestic, holding no intercourse with anyone on board the ship, and yet spreading their wings above her day and night for hundreds of miles over the ocean, with folded feet, the huge white pinions, except for an occasional flap, outstretched in steady sail, never resting, and seemingly never weary, they looked like guardian angels keeping watch over the crew."

"I wonder if they are sorry for the ships that go down?" said Ida, thoughtfully.

Mrs. Overtheway took her hand.

"Do you think it unkind in me to talk of ships, my love?" she asked.

"No, no, no!" Ida exclaimed, "I don't mind *your* talking about it. I wish I could talk to the birds that saw papa's ship go down, if there were any, and ask them how it was, and if he minded it much, and if he remembered me. I used to wish I had been with him, and one night I dreamed about it; but when the water touched me, I was frightened, and screamed, and woke; and then I was glad I hadn't been there, for perhaps he wouldn't have loved me so much if he had seen that I wasn't brave."

The little old lady kissed her tenderly.

"And now the story, please," said Ida, after a pause.

And Mrs. Overtheway began the following story:

KERGUELEN'S LAND

'"Down in the deep, with freight and crew,
Past any help she lies,
And never a bale has come to shore
Of all thy merchandise.

'For cloth o' gold and comely frieze,'
Winstanley said, and sigh'd,
'For velvet coif, or costly coat,
They fathoms deep may bide.

'O thou, brave skipper, blithe and kind,
O mariners bold and true,
Sorry at heart, right sorry am I,
A-thinking of yours and you.'"

—"WINSTANLEY" (JEAN INGELOW)

"Father Albatross had been out all day, and was come home
to the island which gives its name to this story. He had only
taken a short flight, for his wife was hatching an egg, and he
kept comparatively near the island where her nest was
situated. There was only one egg, but parental affection is
not influenced by numbers. There is always love enough for
the largest family, and everything that could be desired in an

only child, and Mother Albatross was as proud as if she had been a hen sitting on a dozen.

"The Father Albatross was very considerate. Not only did he deny himself those long flights which he and his mate had before so greatly enjoyed, but he generally contrived to bring back from his shorter trips some bits of news for her amusement. Their island home lay far out of the common track of ships, but sometimes he sighted a distant vessel, and he generally found something to tell of birds or fish, whales or waterspouts, icebergs or storms. When there was no news he discussed the winds and waves, as we talk of the weather and the crops.

"Bits of news, like misfortunes, are apt to come together. The very day on which the egg hatched, Father Albatross returned from his morning flight so full of what he had seen, that he hardly paid any attention to his mate's announcement of the addition to his family.

"'Could you leave the nest for a quarter of an hour, my dear?' he asked."

"'Certainly not,' said Mother Albatross; 'as I have told you, the egg is hatched at last.'"

"'These things always happen at the least convenient moments,' said the father bird. 'There's a ship within a mere wing-stretch, untold miles out of her course, and going down. I came away just as she was sinking, that you might have a chance of seeing her. It is a horrible sight.'"

"'It must be terrible to witness', she replied, 'and I would give worlds to see it; but a mother's first duty is the nest, and it is quite impossible for me to move. At the same time I beg that you will return, and see whatever there is to be seen.'"

Juliana Horatia Ewing

"'It is not worth while,' he answered; 'there was not a moment to lose, and by this time she must be at the bottom with all belonging to her.'"

"'Could none of them fly away?' the Mother Albatross asked."

"'No men have wings,' replied her mate, 'nor, for that matter, fins or scales either. They are very curious creatures. The fancy they have for wandering about between sea and sky, when Nature has not enabled them to support themselves in either, is truly wonderful. Go where you will over the ocean and you meet men, as you meet fish and birds. Then if anything disables these ships that they contrive to go about in, down they go, and as the men can neither float nor fly, they sink to the bottom like so many stones.'"

"'Were there many on the ship you saw?' the mother bird asked."

"'More than one likes to see drowned in a batch,' said Father Albatross 'and I feel most sorry for the captain. He was a fine fellow, with bright eyes and dark curly plumage, and would have been a handsome creature if he had had wings. He was going about giving orders with desperate and vain composure, and wherever he went there went with him a large dog with dark bright curls like his own. I have seen the ship before, and I know the dog. His name is Carlo. He is the captain's property, and the ship's pet. Usually he is very quiet, and sometimes, when it blows, he is ill; but commonly he was on deck, blinking with the most self-sufficient air you can imagine. However, to-day, from the moment that danger was imminent, he seemed to be aware of it, and to have only one idea on the subject, to keep close to his master. He got in front of him as he moved about, sat down at his feet when he stood still, jumped on him when he shouted his orders, and licked his hands when he seized the ropes. In fact, he was most troublesome. But what can you expect of a creature that requires four legs to go about with, and can't rise above the earth even with these, and doesn't move as many yards in a day as I go miles in an hour? He *can* swim, but only for a certain length of time. However, he is probably quiet enough now; and perhaps some lucky chance has rolled him to his master's feet below the sea.'"

"'Have men no contrivance for escaping on these occasions?' the mother bird inquired."

"'They have boats, into which they go when the ship will hold them no longer. It is much as if you should put out the little one to fly in a storm against which your own wings failed.'"

"'Perhaps the boats are in good order when the ship is not,' said Mother Albatross, who had a practical gift. 'Were there boats to this one?'"

"'There were. I saw one lowered, and quickly filled with men, eager to snatch this last chance of life.

"'Was the captain in it?' she asked."

"'No. He stayed on the ship and gave orders. The dog stayed with him. Another boat was lowered and filled just as the ship went down.'"

"'Was the captain in it?'"

"'Again, no. He stayed with the vessel and some others with him. They were just sinking as I came for you. With the last glance I gave I saw the captain standing quite still near the wheel. The dog was sitting on his feet. They were both looking in one direction—away over the sea. But why should you distress yourself? It is all over long since. Think of the little one, and let us be thankful that we belong to a superior race. We might have been born without wings, like poor sailors.'"

"'I cannot help grieving for the captain,' said Mother Albatross. 'When you spoke of his bright eyes and handsome plumage I thought of you; and how should I feel if you were to die? I wish he had gone in the boats.'"

"'I doubt if he would have fared better,' said the father bird. 'The second boat must have been swamped in the sinking of the ship; and it is far from probable that the other will get to land.'"

"'Nevertheless, I hope you will fly in that direction to-morrow,' she said, 'and bring me word whether there are any traces of the catastrophe.'"

"The following morning Father Albatross set off as he was desired. The ship had foundered quite near to the other side of the island, and including a little excursion to see if the first boat were still above water, he expected to be back very shortly.

"He returned even sooner than the Mother Albatross had hoped, and descended to the side of their nest with as much agitation as his majestic form was capable of displaying.

"'Wonders will never cease!' he exclaimed. 'What do you think are on the island?'"

"'I couldn't guess if I were to try from now till next hatching season,' said his mate; 'and I beg you will not keep me in suspense. I am not equal to the slightest trial of the nerves. It is quite enough to be a mother.'"

"'The captain and one or two more men are here,' said the albatross. 'What do you think of that? You will be able to see him for yourself, and show the youngster what men are like into the bargain. It's very strange how they have escaped; and that lazy, self-sufficient dog is with them.'"

"'I cannot possibly leave our young one at present,' said the Mother Albatross, 'and he certainly cannot get so far. It will be very provoking if the men leave the island before I can see them.'"

"'There is not much to fear of that,' her mate answered. 'A lucky wave has brought them to shore, but it will take a good many lucky waves to bring a ship to carry them home.'"

"Father Albatross was right; but his mate saw the strangers sooner than she expected. Her nest, though built on the ground, was on the highest point of the island, and to this the shipwrecked men soon made their way; and there the Mother Albatross had ample chance of seeing the bright eyes of the captain as they scanned the horizon line with keen anxiety. Presently they fell upon the bird herself.

"'What splendid creatures they are!' he said to his companion; 'and so grandly fearless. I was never on one of these islands where they breed before. What a pity it is that they cannot understand one! That fellow there, who is just stretching his noble wings, might take a message and bring us help.'"

"'He is a fine creature,' said the Mother Albatross, peeping at the captain from her nest; 'that is, he would be if he had wings, and could speak properly, instead of making that unmusical jabbering like a monkey.'"

"'I would give a good deal to one of them for a report of the first boat,' the captain went on. 'Heaven knows I would be content to die here if I could know that it was safe. But I'm afraid—I'm afraid; oh! dear!'"

"And the captain paced up and down, the other consoling him."

"'He doesn't seem as tame as one might expect,' said the Mother Albatross, 'he's so restless. But possibly he is hungry.'"

"Truly it was a great amusement for the mother bird to watch the strangers from her nest, and to question her mate on their peculiarities."

"'What is he doing now?' she asked on one occasion, when the captain was reading a paper which he had taken from the note-book in his pocket."

"'That is a letter,' said the Father Albatross. 'And from the look of it I gather that, like ourselves, he has got a young one somewhere, wherever his nest may be.'"

"'How do you gather that?' his mate inquired."

"'Because the writing is so large,' answered the Father Albatross. 'It is one of the peculiarities of these creatures that the smaller they are the larger they write. That letter is from a young one; probably his own.'"

"'Very remarkable indeed,' said the Mother Albatross. 'And what is he doing now?'"

"'Now he is writing himself,' said her mate; 'and if you observe you will see my statement confirmed. See how much smaller he writes!'"

"The captain had indeed torn a sheet from his note-book, and was busy scribbling upon his knees. Whether the sight of papers was a familiar memory with Carlo, or whether he was merely moved by one of those doggish impulses we so little understand, it is impossible to say; but when the captain began to write, Carlo began to wag his tail, and he wagged it without pause or weariness till the captain had finished, keeping his nearest eye half open, and fixed upon the paper and the captain's moving hand. Once he sat up on his haunches and put his nose on the letter.

"'That is right, old fellow, kiss it,' said the captain. 'I am just telling her about you. Heaven send she may ever read it, poor child!'"

"At this Carlo became so frantic, and so persistent in pushing his nose on to the paper, that the captain was fain to pocket his writing materials, and have a game at play with the 'ship's dog,' in which the latter condescendingly joined for a few minutes, and then lay down as before, shutting his eyes with an air which seemed to imply—

"'I see, poor fellow, you don't understand me.'"

"The hardships endured by this small remnant of the ship's company were not very great. They managed to live. The weather was fine, and they did not at first trouble themselves about any permanent shelter. Perhaps, too, in spite of their seaman's knowledge of the position they were in, some dim hope of a ship out of her course as they had been, picking them off, buoyed them up with the fancy that 'it was not worth while.' But no ship appeared; and they built themselves a hut near the albatross's nest, and began to talk of other seasons, and provision for the future. They kept a look-out by turns through the daylight, and by night when the moon and stars made the distance visible. Every morning the sun rising above the sea met the captain's keen eyes scanning the horizon, and every evening that closed a day's fruitless watch, the sun's going down saw the captain's brown hands clasped together as he said, 'God's will be done!'"

"So days became weeks, and weeks ripened into months, and Carlo became used to his new home, and happy in it, and kept watch over his master, and took his ease as usual. But the men's appearance changed, and their clothes began to look shabby. In the first place they were wearing out, and, secondly, they seemed—as we say—to be 'getting too large' for them, and to hang loosely and untidily upon their gaunt frames. The captain's eyes looked larger and sadder, and his voice grew hollow at sunset, and threads of white began to show among his dark curls, and increased in number day by day.

"'His plumage will be as white as your own very soon,' said the Mother Albatross. 'I suppose it's the climate that does it.'"

"'He is getting older,' said her mate; 'men, like ourselves, get white as they get old.'"

"'But he has been here so short a time,' said Mother Albatross."

"'He is so much the older, however,' said the father bird, and his mate said no more; for she knew by the tone of his voice when he had got to the end of his available information on any subject, and that beyond this point he did not like to be pressed.

"'It's hard, it's very hard, captain, and I can't submit as you do,' said one of the men one day. He and the captain were sitting side by side at the look out, their elbows on their knees, and their chins upon their hands.

"'And yet it's harder for me than for you,' said the captain. 'One must die some day. It's not that. And you are a single man, Barker, without ties.'"

"The man stooped down, and taking one of Carlo's long ears in his hand, played absently with it, as he said—

"'No, sir. I am not married, it's true, and have no children. I feel for you, sir, from my heart. But in a little house just out of Plymouth, that, God above knows, I can see this moment as clearly as I see you, there's a girl that has either forgotten me, or is breaking as good a heart as ever beat in woman's breast for the man that should have been her husband, and that's fast bound here upon a rock with sea-birds. The Lord knows best, captain, but it comes hard. We all have our troubles, sir.'"

"The captain laid his hand upon his shoulder."

"'Forgive me,' he said. 'God comfort you! God bless you!' And, rising hurriedly, he went forward, the big tears breaking over his cheeks, and sea and sky dancing together before his eyes.

"'What do you dream of at night, Barker?' said the captain, on another day."

"'Home, sir,' said Barker."

"'Strange!' said the captain. 'So do I. In all the time we have been here, I have never once dreamed of this island, or of our day's work, nor even of seeing a sail. I dream of England night after night.'"

"'It's the same with myself, sir,' said Barker. 'I'm in Plymouth half my time, I may say. And off and on I dream of my father's old home in Surrey.'"

"'Are the men going to change their feathers, do you think?' the Mother Albatross inquired of her mate. 'They have a most wretched appearance. Only the dog looks like himself.' (The first excitement of pity and curiosity had subsided, and the good couple were now naturally inclined to be critical.)

"'I detest that dog,' said Father Albatross. 'His idleness and arrogance make me quite sick. I think I want exercise, too, and I mean to have a good flight to-day;' and, spreading his broad wings, the bird sailed away.

"His excursion did not quite dispel his irritability. When he returned, he settled down by the captain, who was sitting listlessly, as usual, with Carlo at his feet.

"'If you would only exert yourself,' began Father Albatross, 'something might come of it. You are getting as bad as the dog. Spread out those arms of yours, and see what you can do with them! If you could only fly a matter of a few miles, you would see a sail—and that's more than we had any reason to expect.'"

"'What can be the matter with the birds to-day?' said the captain, who was in rather an irritable mood himself. 'They are silent enough generally'—for the voice of the albatross is rarely heard at sea.

"'Move your arms, I tell you,' croaked the albatross. 'Up and down—so!—and follow me.'"

"'I shall have the dog going at them next,' muttered the captain. 'Come along, Carlo.' And turning his back on Father Albatross, he moved away.

"'He doesn't understand you,' said the Mother Albatross, who endeavoured, as is proper, to soothe her mate's irritability, and make peace. 'Couldn't you take a message to the ship yourself? It is nothing to your magnificent wings, and it is not his fault, poor creature, that he is not formed like you.'"

"'You speak very sensibly, my dear' said Father Albatross; and once more he took flight over the sea."

"But he returned in even worse mood than before."

"'Nothing can equal the stupidity of human beings,' he observed. 'I addressed myself to the captain. "There's an island with shipwrecked men on it a few miles to the north-east," said I. "We shall see land in about ten days, ma'am," says the captain to a lady on deck. "There's as big a fool as yourself wrecked on an island north-east by north," I cried. "If you had the skill of a sparrow you could see it with your own eyes in five minutes." "It's very remarkable," said the captain, "I never heard one of those albatross make a sound before." "And never will again," said I; "it's a waste of time to talk to you. It won't take long to put you and yours under water like the rest." And away I came.'"

"'I don't understand the cry of human beings myself,' said his mate, 'and I'm rather glad I do not; it would only irritate me. Perhaps he did not understand you.'"

"'They are all stupid alike,' said the father bird; 'but I have done my best, and shall not disturb myself any more.'"

"The captain watched till sunset, and folded his hands, and bent his head as usual, and at last lay down to sleep. He dreamt of England, and of home—of a home that had been his long since, of a young wife, dead years ago. He dreamt that he lay, at early morning, in a sunny room in a little cottage where they had lived, and where, in summer, the morning sun awoke them not much later than the birds. He dreamt that his wife was by him, and that she thought that he was asleep, and that, so thinking, she put her arms round his neck to awaken him—that he lay still, and pretended to be slumbering on, and that, so lying, he saw her face bright with an unearthly beauty, and her eyes fixed on him with such intensity of expression that they held him like a spell. Then he felt her warm face come nearer to his, and she kissed his cheeks, and he heard her say, 'Wake up, my darling, I have something to show you.' Again she repeated vehemently, 'Awake! Awake! Look! Look!' and then he opened his eyes.

"He was lying at the look-out, and Carlo was licking his face. It was a dream, and yet the voice was strong and clear in his ears, 'Awake! Awake! Look! Look!'"

"A heavier hand than his wife's was on his shoulder, and Barker's rough voice (hoarser than usual), repeated the words of his dream."

"The captain's eyes followed the outstretched hand to the horizon; and then his own voice grew hoarse, as he exclaimed—

"'My God! it is a sail!'"

*   *   *   *   *

Ida was not leaning on the little old lady's footstool now. She sat upright, her pale face whiter than its wont.

"*Did* the ship take them away?" she asked eagerly.

"Yes, my dear. Their signals were seen, and the ship took them home to their friends, who had believed them to be dead."

"Do people who have been drowned—I mean who have been thought to be drowned—ever come home *really?*" the child asked.

"Yes, really. Ida, my dear, I want you to remember that, as regards the captain and the crew, this is a true story."

Ida clasped her hands passionately together.

"Oh, Mrs. Overtheway! Do you think Papa will ever come home?"

"My child! my dear child!" sobbed the little old lady. "I think he will." ...

*　*　*　*　*

"And he *is* alive—he is coming home!" Ida cried, as she recounted Mrs. Overtheway's story to Nurse, who knew the principal fact of it already. "And she told it to me in this way not to frighten me. I did cry and laugh though, and was very silly; but she said I must not be foolish, but brave like a captain's daughter, and that I ought to thank GOD for being so good to me, when the children of the other poor men who died will never have their fathers back in this world: and I am thankful, so thankful! Only it is like a mill going in my head, and I cannot help crying. And Papa wrote me a long letter when he was on the island, and he sent it to Mrs. Overtheway because Uncle Garbett told him that I was fond of her, and that she would tell me nicely, and she was to read it, and to give it to me when she had told me. And it is such a lovely letter, with all about the island, and poor Barker, and dear old Carlo, and about the beautiful birds, too, only Mrs. Overtheway made up a great deal of that herself. And please, Nursey, take off my black frock and never let me see it again, for the Captain is really coming home, and, oh! how I

　Juliana Horatia Ewing

wish he would come!"

The poor child was terribly excited, but her habits of obedience stood her in good stead, for though she was vehemently certain that she could not possibly go to sleep, in compliance with Nurse's wishes, she went to bed, and there at last slept heavily and long; so that when she awoke there was only just time to dress and be ready to meet her father. She was putting out her treasures for him to look at, the carved fans and workboxes, the beads and handkerchiefs and feathers, the new letter and the old one—when the Captain came.

* * * * *

A week after the postman had delivered the letter which contained such wonderful news for Ida, he brought another to Mrs. Overtheway's green gate, addressed in the same handwriting—the Captain's. It was not from the Captain, however, but from Ida.

"MY DEAR, DEAR MRS. OVERTHEWAY,

"We got here on Saturday night, and are so happy. Papa says when will you come and see us? I have got a little room to myself, and I have got a glass case under which I keep all the things that Papa ever sent me, and his letters. I bought it with part of a sovereign Uncle Garbett gave me when I came away. Do you know he was so very kind when I came away. He kissed me, and said, 'GOD bless you, my dear! You are a good child, a very good child;' and you know it was very kind of him, for I don't think I ever was good somehow with him. But he was so kind it made me cry, so I couldn't say anything, but I gave him a great many kisses, for I did not want him to know I love Papa the best. Carlo will put his nose on my knee, and I can't help making blots. He came with us in the railway carriage, and ate nearly all my sandwiches. When he and Papa roll on the hearthrug together, I mix their curls up and pretend I can't tell which is which. Only really Papa's have got some grey hairs in them: *we know why*. I always kiss the white hairs when I find them, and he says he thinks I shall kiss the colour into them again. He is so kind! I said I didn't like Nurse to wear her black dress now, and she said it was the best one she had, and she must wear it in the afternoon; so Papa said he would get us all some bright things, for he says English people dress in mud-colour, while people who live in much sunnier, brighter countries wear gay clothes. So we went into a shop this morning, and I asked him to get my things all blue, because it is his favourite colour. But he said he should choose Nurse's things himself. So he asked for a very smart dress, and the man asked what kind; and I said it was for a nurse, so he brought out a lot of prints, and at last Papa chose one with a yellow ground and carnations on it. He wanted very much to have got another one with very big flowers, but the man said it was meant for curtains, not for dresses, so I persuaded him not to get it; but he says now he wishes he had, as it was much the best. Then he got a red shawl, and a bonnet ribbon of a kind of green tartan. Nurse was very much pleased, but she said they were too smart by half. But Papa told her it was because she knew no better, and had never seen the parrots in the East Indian Islands. Yesterday we all went to church. Carlo came too, and when we got to the porch, Papa put up his hand, and said, 'Prayers, sir!' and Carlo lay down and stayed there till we came out. Papa says that he used to do so when he was going to say prayers on board ship, and that Carlo always lay quietly on deck till the service was over. Before we went to church Papa gave me a little parcel sealed up, to put in the plate. I asked him what it was, and he said it was a thank offering. Before

Juliana Horatia Ewing

one of the prayers the clergyman said something. I don't quite remember the words, but it began, 'A sailor desires to thank GOD—' and oh! I *knew* who it was, and I squeezed his hand very tight, and I tried to pray every word of that prayer, only once I began to think of the island—but I *did* try! And indeed I do try to be very, very thankful, for I am so very happy! Papa got a letter from Barker this morning, and we are going out to choose him a wedding present. He sent a photograph of the girl he is going to marry, and I was rather disappointed, for I thought she would be very lovely, only, perhaps, rather sad-looking; but she doesn't look very pretty, and is sitting in rather a vulgar dress, with a photograph book in her hand. Her dress is tartan, and queer-looking about the waist, you know, like Nurse's, and it is coloured in the picture, and her brooch is gilt. Papa laughs, and says Barker likes colour, as he does; and he says he thinks she has a nice face, and he knows she is very good, and very fond of Barker, and that Barker thinks her beautiful. He didn't write before he went to see her, like Papa. He just walked up to the house, and found her sitting at the window with his photograph in her hand. She said she had been so restless all day, she could do nothing but sit and look at it. Wasn't it funny? She had been very ill with thinking he was dead, and Barker says she nearly died of the joy of seeing him again. Papa sends you his love, and I send lots and lots of mine, and millions of kisses. And please, *please* come and see us if you can, for I miss you every morning, and I do love you, and am always your grateful and affectionate

"IDA."

"P.S.—I am telling Papa all your stories by bits. And do you know he went to sleep whilst I was telling him Mrs. Moss!"

Chim! chime! chim! chime! chim! chime!

The story is ended, but the bells still call to Morning Prayer, and life goes on. The little old lady comes through the green gate, and looks over the way, but there is no face at that window now; something in it made her start for an instant, but it is only a looking-glass, for the smart toilette-table has been brought back to the window where Ida used to kneel, and the nursery is a spare bedroom once more. That episode in this dull house in the quiet street is over, and gone by. The old lady thinks so rather sadly as she goes where the bells are calling. The pale, eager, loving little face that turned to her in its loneliness, now brightens a happy home; but the remembrance of it is with the little old lady still, pleasant as the remembrance of flowers when winter has come. Yes, truly, not the least pleasant of Mrs. Overtheway's Remembrances.

Juliana Horatia Ewing

Choose from Thousands of 1stWorldLibrary Classics By

A. M. Barnard
Ada Leverson
Adolphus William Ward
Aesop
Agatha Christie
Alexander Aaronsohn
Alexander Kielland
Alexandre Dumas
Alfred Gatty
Alfred Ollivant
Alice Duer Miller
Alice Turner Curtis
Alice Dunbar
Allen Chapman
Alleyne Ireland
Ambrose Bierce
Amelia E. Barr
Amory H. Bradford
Andrew Lang
Andrew McFarland Davis
Andy Adams
Angela Brazil
Anna Alice Chapin
Anna Sewell
Annie Besant
Annie Hamilton Donnell
Annie Payson Call
Annie Roe Carr
Annonaymous
Anton Chekhov
Archibald Lee Fletcher
Arnold Bennett
Arthur C. Benson
Arthur Conan Doyle
Arthur M. Winfield
Arthur Ransome
Arthur Schnitzler
Arthur Train
Atticus
B.H. Baden-Powell
B. M. Bower
B. C. Chatterjee
Baroness Emmuska Orczy
Baroness Orczy
Basil King
Bayard Taylor
Ben Macomber
Bertha Muzzy Bower
Bjornstjerne Bjornson

Booth Tarkington
Boyd Cable
Bram Stoker
C. Collodi
C. E. Orr
C. M. Ingleby
Carolyn Wells
Catherine Parr Traill
Charles A. Eastman
Charles Amory Beach
Charles Dickens
Charles Dudley Warner
Charles Farrar Browne
Charles Ives
Charles Kingsley
Charles Klein
Charles Hanson Towne
Charles Lathrop Pack
Charles Romyn Dake
Charles Whibley
Charles Willing Beale
Charlotte M. Braeme
Charlotte M. Yonge
Charlotte Perkins Stetson
Clair W. Hayes
Clarence Day Jr.
Clarence E. Mulford
Clemence Housman
Confucius
Coningsby Dawson
Cornelis DeWitt Wilcox
Cyril Burleigh
D. H. Lawrence
Daniel Defoe
David Garnett
Dinah Craik
Don Carlos Janes
Donald Keyhoe
Dorothy Kilner
Dougan Clark
Douglas Fairbanks
E. Nesbit
E. P. Roe
E. Phillips Oppenheim
E. S. Brooks
Earl Barnes
Edgar Rice Burroughs
Edith Van Dyne
Edith Wharton

Edward Everett Hale
Edward J. O'Biren
Edward S. Ellis
Edwin L. Arnold
Eleanor Atkins
Eleanor Hallowell Abbott
Eliot Gregory
Elizabeth Gaskell
Elizabeth McCracken
Elizabeth Von Arnim
Ellem Key
Emerson Hough
Emilie F. Carlen
Emily Bronte
Emily Dickinson
Enid Bagnold
Enilor Macartney Lane
Erasmus W. Jones
Ernie Howard Pie
Ethel May Dell
Ethel Turner
Ethel Watts Mumford
Eugene Sue
Eugenie Foa
Eugene Wood
Eustace Hale Ball
Evelyn Everett-green
Everard Cotes
F. H. Cheley
F. J. Cross
F. Marion Crawford
Fannie E. Newberry
Federick Austin Ogg
Ferdinand Ossendowski
Fergus Hume
Florence A. Kilpatrick
Fremont B. Deering
Francis Bacon
Francis Darwin
Frances Hodgson Burnett
Frances Parkinson Keyes
Frank Gee Patchin
Frank Harris
Frank Jewett Mather
Frank L. Packard
Frank V. Webster
Frederic Stewart Isham
Frederick Trevor Hill
Frederick Winslow Taylor

Friedrich Kerst
Friedrich Nietzsche
Fyodor Dostoyevsky
G.A. Henty
G.K. Chesterton
Gabrielle E. Jackson
Garrett P. Serviss
Gaston Leroux
George A. Warren
George Ade
Geroge Bernard Shaw
George Cary Eggleston
George Durston
George Ebers
George Eliot
George Gissing
George MacDonald
George Meredith
George Orwell
George Sylvester Viereck
George Tucker
George W. Cable
George Wharton James
Gertrude Atherton
Gordon Casserly
Grace E. King
Grace Gallatin
Grace Greenwood
Grant Allen
Guillermo A. Sherwell
Gulielma Zollinger
Gustav Flaubert
H. A. Cody
H. B. Irving
H.C. Bailey
H. G. Wells
H. H. Munro
H. Irving Hancock
H. R. Naylor
H. Rider Haggard
H. W. C. Davis
Haldeman Julius
Hall Caine
Hamilton Wright Mabie
Hans Christian Andersen
Harold Avery
Harold McGrath
Harriet Beecher Stowe
Harry Castlemon
Harry Coghill
Harry Houidini

Hayden Carruth
Helent Hunt Jackson
Helen Nicolay
Hendrik Conscience
Hendy David Thoreau
Henri Barbusse
Henrik Ibsen
Henry Adams
Henry Ford
Henry Frost
Henry James
Henry Jones Ford
Henry Seton Merriman
Henry W Longfellow
Herbert A. Giles
Herbert Carter
Herbert N. Casson
Herman Hesse
Hildegard G. Frey
Homer
Honore De Balzac
Horace B. Day
Horace Walpole
Horatio Alger Jr.
Howard Pyle
Howard R. Garis
Hugh Lofting
Hugh Walpole
Humphry Ward
Ian Maclaren
Inez Haynes Gillmore
Irving Bacheller
Isabel Cecilia Williams
Isabel Hornibrook
Israel Abrahams
Ivan Turgenev
J.G.Austin
J. Henri Fabre
J. M. Barrie
J. M. Walsh
J. Macdonald Oxley
J. R. Miller
J. S. Fletcher
J. S. Knowles
J. Storer Clouston
J. W. Duffield
Jack London
Jacob Abbott
James Allen
James Andrews
James Baldwin

James Branch Cabell
James DeMille
James Joyce
James Lane Allen
James Lane Allen
James Oliver Curwood
James Oppenheim
James Otis
James R. Driscoll
Jane Abbott
Jane Austen
Jane L. Stewart
Janet Aldridge
Jens Peter Jacobsen
Jerome K. Jerome
Jessie Graham Flower
John Buchan
John Burroughs
John Cournos
John F. Kennedy
John Gay
John Glasworthy
John Habberton
John Joy Bell
John Kendrick Bangs
John Milton
John Philip Sousa
John Taintor Foote
Jonas Lauritz Idemil Lie
Jonathan Swift
Joseph A. Altsheler
Joseph Carey
Joseph Conrad
Joseph E. Badger Jr
Joseph Hergesheimer
Joseph Jacobs
Jules Vernes
Julian Hawthrone
Julie A Lippmann
Justin Huntly McCarthy
Kakuzo Okakura
Karle Wilson Baker
Kate Chopin
Kenneth Grahame
Kenneth McGaffey
Kate Langley Bosher
Kate Langley Bosher
Katherine Cecil Thurston
Katherine Stokes
L. A. Abbot
L. T. Meade

L. Frank Baum
Latta Griswold
Laura Dent Crane
Laura Lee Hope
Laurence Housman
Lawrence Beasley
Leo Tolstoy
Leonid Andreyev
Lewis Carroll
Lewis Sperry Chafer
Lilian Bell
Lloyd Osbourne
Louis Hughes
Louis Joseph Vance
Louis Tracy
Louisa May Alcott
Lucy Fitch Perkins
Lucy Maud Montgomery
Luther Benson
Lydia Miller Middleton
Lyndon Orr
M. Corvus
M. H. Adams
Margaret E. Sangster
Margret Howth
Margaret Vandercook
Margaret W. Hungerford
Margret Penrose
Maria Edgeworth
Maria Thompson Daviess
Mariano Azuela
Marion Polk Angellotti
Mark Overton
Mark Twain
Mary Austin
Mary Catherine Crowley
Mary Cole
Mary Hastings Bradley
Mary Roberts Rinehart
Mary Rowlandson
M. Wollstonecraft Shelley
Maud Lindsay
Max Beerbohm
Myra Kelly
Nathaniel Hawthrone
Nicolo Machiavelli
O. F. Walton
Oscar Wilde

Owen Johnson
P.G. Wodehouse
Paul and Mabel Thorne
Paul G. Tomlinson
Paul Severing
Percy Brebner
Percy Keese Fitzhugh
Peter B. Kyne
Plato
Quincy Allen
R. Derby Holmes
R. L. Stevenson
R. S. Ball
Rabindranath Tagore
Rahul Alvares
Ralph Bonehill
Ralph Henry Barbour
Ralph Victor
Ralph Waldo Emmerson
Rene Descartes
Ray Cummings
Rex Beach
Rex E. Beach
Richard Harding Davis
Richard Jefferies
Richard Le Gallienne
Robert Barr
Robert Frost
Robert Gordon Anderson
Robert L. Drake
Robert Lansing
Robert Lynd
Robert Michael Ballantyne
Robert W. Chambers
Rosa Nouchette Carey
Rudyard Kipling
Saint Augustine
Samuel B. Allison
Samuel Hopkins Adams
Sarah Bernhardt
Sarah C. Hallowell
Selma Lagerlof
Sherwood Anderson
Sigmund Freud
Standish O'Grady
Stanley Weyman
Stella Benson
Stella M. Francis

Stephen Crane
Stewart Edward White
Stijn Streuvels
Swami Abhedananda
Swami Parmananda
T. S. Ackland
T. S. Arthur
The Princess Der Ling
Thomas A. Janvier
Thomas A Kempis
Thomas Anderton
Thomas Bailey Aldrich
Thomas Bulfinch
Thomas De Quincey
Thomas Dixon
Thomas H. Huxley
Thomas Hardy
Thomas More
Thornton W. Burgess
U. S. Grant
Upton Sinclair
Valentine Williams
Various Authors
Vaughan Kester
Victor Appleton
Victor G. Durham
Victoria Cross
Virginia Woolf
Wadsworth Camp
Walter Camp
Walter Scott
Washington Irving
Wilbur Lawton
Wilkie Collins
Willa Cather
Willard F. Baker
William Dean Howells
William le Queux
W. Makepeace Thackeray
William W. Walter
William Shakespeare
Winston Churchill
Yei Theodora Ozaki
Yogi Ramacharaka
Young E. Allison
Zane Grey